FROM ATHEISM
TO ETERNAL LIFE

Proof that You Can Live Forever

Mark D. Taylor

Eternity Books, LLC
Villa Ridge, Missouri

From Atheism to Eternal Life: Proof that You Can Live Forever

by Mark D. Taylor

Copyright © 2014 by Eternity Books, LLC
All Rights Reserved
ISBN-13: 978-1500606350
ISBN-10: 1500606359

Published by: Eternity Books, LLC

Cover Photos:
Background photo is by NASA/Ames Research Center,
courtesy of nasaimages.org
Foreground photo is a NASA public-domain image

Unless otherwise indicated,
Scripture quotations taken from
the New American Standard Bible®,
Copyright © 1960, 1962, 1963, 1968, 1971, 1972, 1973,
1975, 1977, 1995 by The Lockman Foundation
Used by permission." (www.Lockman.org)

Scripture quotations marked NIV are taken from the Holy Bible, New International Version®, NIV®. Copyright © 1973, 1978, 1984 by Biblica, Inc.™ Used by permission of Zondervan. All rights reserved worldwide. (www.zondervan.com)

To Ruth

My Wife, Companion, and Best Friend for the last 28 years

Contacting the Author

I would love to hear from you and continue the dialogue regarding eternal truth. Please visit the web-site for this book, to send me your thoughts and questions or to see additional information. You can also obtain a free audio version of the book:

www.eternitybook.org

Table of Contents

ACKNOWLEDGMENTS	VI
INTRODUCTION	1
PART 1: THE EXISTENCE OF GOD	**5**
THE ORIGIN OF THE UNIVERSE	6
ATHEISM AND ETERNITY-PAST	13
A RATIONAL EXPLANATION FOR THE UNIVERSE	24
GOD AND ETERNITY-PAST	31
INTENTIONAL EVIDENCE	38
PART 2: INFINITE VALUE	**42**
PHILOSOPHIES THAT IGNORE ETERNITY	43
THE INFINITE VALUE OF ETERNAL LIFE	50
PART 3: THE REVELATION OF TRUTH	**57**
FAITH AND REVELATION	58
THE REVELATION OF TRUTH	67
FULFILLED PROPHECIES	80
PART 4: ETERNITY-FUTURE	**98**
THE BOOK FROM GOD	99
THE ETERNAL PERSON	101
ETERNITY-FUTURE	104
ENTERING ETERNAL LIFE	113
BIBLIOGRAPHY	121
NOTES	124

Acknowledgments

While in high school, I desired an intellectual framework which would integrate reason, faith, and science. I then stepped into the classroom of Dr. David Neuhouser at Taylor University. In a series of classes called "Ways of Knowing", he presented the various tools and sources whereby the human mind learns about reality, and helped us apply those methods for a rational understanding of eternal truth. I highly recommend his book <u>Open to Reason</u> (Taylor University Press), and in some ways the book that I have written is an implementation of the concepts presented in Part 1 of that book.

In addition, while at Taylor University I was introduced to and stimulated by the writings of C. S. Lewis and other excellent authors in the area of faith and reason. I have been especially influenced by Francis Schaeffer's reasoning, style, and compassion. I was privileged to hear him speak at Taylor University shortly before his death. I will never forget the moment when a packed auditorium sat waiting to see him, and then the curtains were pulled back to reveal a very ill man lying on a bed. He was literally on his deathbed, but decided it was important to come and share his thoughts with a young group of inquiring minds before leaving this life behind.

My wonderful wife Ruth has been very supportive and has allowed many things to be placed on low priority while I have worked on the book. My mom has given the book a thorough critique in grammar and punctuation. My sons Matthew and Daniel have also been very encouraging for the project. My brother Scott has influenced some of the logical reasoning. My sister-in-law Michelle, and parents-in-law John and Norma Dearden, have been supportive.

Several friends have had a large impact on my understanding of eternal truth. Daryl Lynn has taught me to treasure God's revelation of truth, to study it enthusiastically, and to trust its promises. He has also provided encouragement and suggestions for this book. Dale Rhoton provided valuable encouragement at a crucial time, and has also been an example of a loving and humble approach to those seeking truth. Eric Lynn provided some important suggestions for the book.

Many other friends have given detailed reviews and suggestions, especially Dr. Marvin Bittinger, Steve Lightfoot, Tim Butler, Andy Tash, Mary Taylor, and Kathy Herman. Matt Davids provided the general cover design as well as some valuable suggestions. Some others who have also given helpful input are Johnny Suermann, Cordell Schulten, Ed Sewell, John Rhoton, Doug Roth, Natalie Plakhova, Dr. Jim Spiegel, Brad Keating, Elijah Keating, Dan Butts, Terry Pabst, Eric Bruder, Sam Collins, and Todd Proctor. Many friends and relatives, such as Jeff McNeal, Barb Kryvko, Joe Jacob, Macie Santschi, D.J. Lynn, Matt McKee, Tim McNeal, Eric Darrough, Rick Orr, and Andrew Davis, have also provided encouragement along the journey. Zach Lynn and Micah Lynn have developed a web-site for the book, which is at www.eternitybook.org.

Randy Amos provided valuable insight through his teaching at a conference at Turkey Hill Ranch Bible Camp. He presented some key concepts regarding the verification of supernatural revelation, which is described in Chapter 9.

Mark Taylor
Villa Ridge, Missouri
August, 2014

Introduction

Perhaps this morning you browsed the Internet, had breakfast with your family, and then went to work or school. You spent the day with friends and co-workers, and your time was filled with thinking, talking, walking, and eating. You experienced joys, disappointments, deep thoughts, and physical pleasures.

Most leading atheists claim that your personal life is part of a temporary reality which suddenly appeared out of complete nothingness. Have you ever questioned whether that is true?

As for the future, science tells us that the universe and everything in it is running down. Does this mean that you, your family, your friends, and all life will eventually cease to exist forever?

Is everything in our lives simply the result of a temporary cosmic accident? In short, did all that we see and experience come "from nothing" and will eventually go back "to nothing"?

Rather than asserting that "everything is temporary", we will search whether "something is permanent". As shown in the following diagram, I would like to suggest that there are actually two realities, one physical and the other invisible yet permanent:

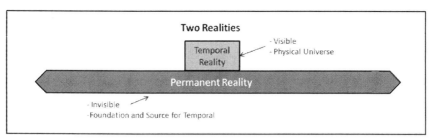

Figure 1

<u>We will consider whether the separate eternal reality exists, and whether it is actually the source of our own temporary reality.</u>

The ultimate foundation of our physical universe is either nothingness or an eternal, supernatural source. Nothingness implies that value and meaning are hopeful inventions, but a supernatural source can perhaps provide a rational basis for order, purpose, and lasting happiness.

Personally, I am a Christian and have always had a desire for an understanding of eternity which is based on an intellectual foundation, and not merely on blind faith. I place high value on logical reasoning, which is heavily influenced by my own background in both mathematics and computer science. Presented here is an end-to-end logical framework which fulfills my own quest.

A Common Framework for Absolute Truth

When an atheist and a Christian discuss the existence of God, they can become frustrated trying to bridge the gap between the physical universe and anything supernatural. The atheist wants rational discussion to be limited to the boundaries of the universe, and feels that the Christian is getting religious and irrational each time he talks about God. The Christian often asks the atheist to make a leap of faith to the supernatural.

We can benefit from a reasoned approach which starts with the physical and proceeds logically to the supernatural in an unbroken chain. A rational way to perform this transition is to start with the beginning of the universe and proceed backward to the infinite past. Moreover, the infinite past can become a foundation for considering the infinite future and the possibility of personal eternal life.

Leading atheists claim they are searching for absolute truth and a "Theory of Everything", but most of them ignore eternity. Their theories sometimes takes us to the "edge" of the origin of the universe, but rarely attempt to carry us over to what was beyond the edge.

Only a willingness to examine eternity will lead to reasonable conclusions regarding permanent truth. A relative and temporal approach to truth is inherently limited and cannot lead to sufficient answers. We will discuss a systematic method not only for exploring the existence of God, but also for investigating several attributes of His nature. This method is based solely on scientific principles and deductive reasoning.

I am treating "truth" as knowledge which is absolute and in accordance with reality, not as that which is merely useful and subjective. As David Neuhouser humorously points out in <u>Open to Reason</u>, *"Truth might be defined as whatever does not disturb what we already believe"*.[1] However, despite the fact that human nature can indeed create resistance to changing our views, I think that most of us realize we <u>should</u> be seeking to improve our understanding of reality in a reasoned manner. Looking into eternal matters requires such openness, and is most sensibly approached with an actual desire to know truth.

The Infinite Value of Eternal Life

The difference in consequences between atheism and the existence of a loving God are enormous, and we will examine the comparative value for humanity as well as our own personal destiny. The atheist Michel de Montaigne proclaimed, *"Live as long as you please, you will strike nothing off the time you will have to spend dead"*.[2] In contrast to this, the Bible asks us to *"take hold of the eternal life to which you were called" (1 Timothy 6:12).*

The infinite value of eternal life does not prove that God exists, but it should motivate us to diligently search for the truth. It is my sincere hope that this book will help with that search. If there is a way to obtain eternal life but we do not find it, then we have committed a mistake with catastrophic results and the loss of an enormous opportunity.

I encourage you to read through the entire book in a single sitting, if possible. The four parts and thirteen chapters are laid out in a logical sequence which ends with the way to obtain eternal life.

> *Note: Although the Bible is quoted a few times in the early part of the book, I am not at this point treating it as a source of knowledge. The quotes are just intended to highlight its correspondence with our reasoning and conclusions. Later in the book (chapters 8-10) we will investigate whether the Bible is a trustworthy source of truth.*

Part 1: The Existence of God

| Existence of God | Infinite Value | Revelation of Truth | Eternity Future |

Chapter 1
The Origin of the Universe

Are all things temporary, or is something permanent?

An appropriate study for ultimate reality is the context of the universe in relation to eternity, as shown in the following diagram.

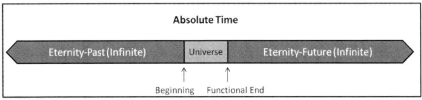

Figure 2

We should look at the big picture, which includes *(1) an infinite amount of time in the past, (2) the beginning, duration, and termination of our physical universe, and (3) an infinite amount of time yet to come.* Contrary to what many people think, the Bible agrees with such a reasoned and scientific approach:

> ...while we look not at the things which are seen, but at the things which are not seen; <u>for the things which are seen are temporal, but the things which are not seen are eternal.</u> (2 Corinthians 4:18)

This is not a statement of religion, but of time, existence, and reality. It raises the possibility that there are actually two realities: the "Temporal Reality" in which we live, and the "Permanent Reality" which has always existed. It is useful to distinguish between these, and to focus our attention on determining what things are truly permanent, even though they might be invisible to us at this current time. Science affirms that most of the things that we see on a daily basis are actually temporary.

Most leading atheists hold to a limited view of time. In regard to the past, they contend that the beginning of everything occurred about 14 billion years ago. In regard to the future, the law of entropy (increasing disorder) inevitably leads to a conclusion in which there will be a complete end of life and a functional collapse of the universe in a finite number of years. Atheism infers that our physical lives and ordered universe are simply a temporary lucky accident which will eventually end. As stated by the atheist Sam Harris:

> *"We live in a world where all things, good and bad, are finally destroyed by change... This life, when surveyed with a broad glance, presents little more than a vast spectacle of loss." (Sam Harris, The End of Faith)*[3]

The usual atheistic answer for the ultimate origin of everything physical is essentially, "Nothing", asserting that it happened without any pre-existing building blocks, causes, or laws (this will be examined in chapter 2). However, even leading atheist-or-agnostic Stephen Hawking admits the following:

> *"...it is not only the peculiar characteristics of our solar system that seem oddly conducive to the development of human life but also the characteristics of our entire universe, and that is much more difficult to explain."*
> *(Stephen Hawking, The Grand Design)*[4]

I want to look beyond our temporary age and suggest that history actually has been going on for an infinite amount of time, even though our physical universe (and any other hypothetical universes) did indeed start at a finite point in the past.

Reason tells us there is something that has always been, for there could not have been a point in time at which something came from complete nothingness. If there was a Big Bang, it originated from something that is eternal.

The Options: Source or No Source?

Most discussions and debates regarding the origin of the universe have been focused on what I regard as finite history. However, I believe that compelling answers can be determined through an analysis of eternity-past. The following diagram lays out the major two choices, under a timeline of eternity:

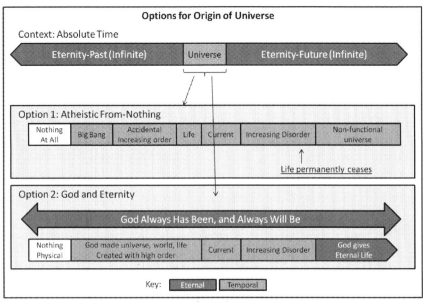

Figure 3

The ultimate origin of everything physical primarily comes down to two alternatives: *(1) there was <u>absolutely nothing</u>, and all of a sudden everything physical appeared; or (2) <u>God has always existed</u>, and at a point in time He created the physical universe.* I believe that the first choice is logically impossible, and the second is logically necessary.

> *Note: A minority of atheists believe that the universe has always existed. Both atheistic options will be discussed in Chapter 2.*

The primary atheistic view ("Option 1") is that there was absolutely nothing, and then the Big Bang event occurred around 14 billion years ago. This was followed by an amazing sequence of increasing order, eventually resulting in life. Life forms also increased in sophistication through a series of accidents. However, the natural law of increasing disorder means that all life will eventually die out, and the universe will finally reach a state of non-functional disorder. Eternity-past and Eternity-future are ignored. This view will be discussed in detail in Chapter 2.

The eternal God view ("Option 2") holds that a supreme being has always existed, apart from the universe or anything physical. At a point in time, He brought physical matter and energy into existence and created the universe. He made the universe with high sophistication, from which it has been decreasing. Since He is eternal and all-powerful, He is able to give people eternal life, which is both physical and spiritual. The eternal and creative attributes of God are explored in Chapter 4.

It is important to emphasize that this view does not hold that God came from nothing at some point, nor that He made Himself. On the contrary, it claims that He has always existed and will continue to exist into the eternal future.

The alternatives of "something-from-nothing" and "an eternal God" can be reasonably analyzed, and then each person can decide in which of these he will place his faith:

> "Ultimately, you choose the faith axioms you trust and follow." (Marvin Bittinger, The Faith Equation)[5]

In addition to the problem of "something-from-nothing", the atheistic option also depends on a long series of lucky accidents, which contradicts the well-established physical law of increasing disorder. The option of an eternal God holds that He is highly intelligent and created a sophisticated universe which has subsequently been running down. Since God is eternal, this option also enables us to search for whether He cares for us and wants to provide us with eternal life.

Time: Absolute versus Operational

Some scientists have suggested that time did not exist before or during the beginning of the universe, and then jump to the radical conclusion that it is, therefore, irrelevant to even discuss how the universe began. [6]

However, it is not valid to say that an event didn't happen or can't be discussed because there might not have been a running clock at the time. We can understand this by distinguishing between two types of time, as shown in the below diagram:

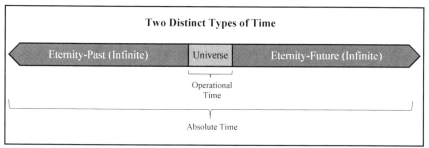

Figure 4

There is a categorical difference between time as an operational mechanism of a system (such as our universe), and the general concept of time as the progression of all existence and events:

- *Absolute time*: Time independent of, and separate from, anything physical; the progression of all existence and events from eternity-past to eternity-future.
- *Operational time*: Time as a relative and integrated dimension within any physical system, such as the universe.

It is a logical fallacy to use these two concepts of time interchangeably for deductions about origins. Let's look at an example to see why this is the case...

Consider the dimension of time in our universe ("operational time") analogous to a computer processing unit, in which an internal clock sends regular pulses to cause the next event to happen. If your laptop has a processor that operates at one gigahertz, this means that the clock sends one billion pulses per second, with an instruction executed for each pulse. This timer is an integral component and dimension of each computer system, similar to the role of time for our own universe.

However, the fact that a computer uses a clock does not mean that "time" did not exist before that computer was manufactured. Similarly, the role in our universe of a measurable aspect of operational time does not mean that nothing was happening or existing before then. Rather than the semantic confusion of "a time when there was no time", we simply need to clarify that general time ("absolute time") was ongoing before the clock-pulse of our universe had started.

The limitations of operational time do not change the fundamental question of ultimate origins: *Did everything physical come from complete nothingness, or was it caused by something pre-existing?* The operational definition of time as a dimension of our universe does nothing to change the questions, alter the discussion, or provide the answers to ultimate origins. In addition, implying that it is unreasonable to discuss ultimate origins is itself a self-contradictory argument and conclusion.

A central point of this book is that it is logically and physically impossible to get something from nothing. Consequently, something has always existed, and there is an eternity-past with an infinite amount of time which has already occurred.

| Existence of God | Infinite Value | Revelation of Truth | Eternity Future |

Chapter 2
Atheism and Eternity-Past

Atheism is logically and physically impossible,
Which is understood through consideration of Eternity-Past.

"The world, then, would not be eternal."
Aristotle

When looking into the true history and ultimate destiny of our universe, a first logical step is to consider whether all that exists is physical. In a scientific and reasoned manner, we can seek to determine whether there is anything supernatural. Since God is not directly seen, many people assume that there is no evidence for His existence. Faith in God is often considered to be a hopeful illusion that has nothing to do with the real, physical universe. Such assumptions cause many scientists to exclude the consideration of God from any discussions about origins of life or the universe.

The "Luck" Assertion

There are several atheistic theories about origins, and it seems to me that they are essentially based on, *"lots of luck, lots of time, and lots of stuff"*. We can see the hopeful confidence in "luck" clearly stated in the striking quote below. This statement is from a leading atheistic-or-agnostic book, right after an explanation of many amazing details of the universe which are absolutely necessary for life:

"What can we make of these coincidences? Luck in the precise form and nature of fundamental physical law is a different kind of luck from the luck we find in environmental factors. It cannot be so easily explained, and has far deeper physical and philosophical implications. Our universe and its laws appear to have a design that both is tailor-made to support us and, if we are to exist, leaves little room for alteration. That is not easily explained, and raises the natural question of why it is that way." (Stephen Hawking, The Grand Design)[7]

I certainly agree with this author that our universe appears to have a "design" that is "tailor-made" to support life, but I don't agree that it is "luck".

Atheistic Options for the Origin of the Universe

This chapter is intended to provide evidence that atheism is logically and physically impossible. The next two chapters then provide evidence that the existence of God is a logical and physical necessity.

The term "eternity-past" refers to an infinite, unlimited amount of time that has already occurred. In other words, "time with no beginning point", but that which has always been. This is certainly a difficult concept for us to grasp, and by its very definition goes beyond, and is even in contradiction to, what we normally understand of the attributes of our temporal physical universe. Nevertheless, it is a concept that we should not ignore or write-off as unreal, for eternity-past is fundamental to a consideration of the present and of the future. In fact, applying our minds to eternity-past can quickly lead us to answers regarding extremely important issues for all people.

Atheism is a statement of what "is not", contending that there is no God. It can also be called "Materialism", as a statement of what "is": only matter, energy, and physical laws. For the purposes of this chapter, materialism can be described as the following:
- Matter and energy are all that has ever existed, or ever will exist;
- There is no supernatural God, never has been, and never will be;
- There is no spiritual world, never has been, and never will be.

An important corollary for Atheism is that "Matter and energy were not brought into existence by anything supernatural". Therefore, when we look at eternity-past from an atheistic viewpoint, there really are only two options for the existence of today's physical universe:
1) Temporal: At some point in time, the physical universe came into existence "from nothing";
2) Eternal: The physical universe has always existed.

When I discuss the universe in this chapter, I am referring to the total package of everything physical (matter and energy) that has ever existed. Some authors such as Stephen Hawking speak of multiple universes, which in total is sometimes called the "multiverse". In regard to that theory, I am talking about the ultimate origin of the entire hypothetical multiverse and any background physical framework.

1. The Atheistic Temporal Option: From Nothing to Something with the Big Bang

Let's first examine what I am calling the "Temporal" option: the physical came from absolutely nothing. This is the viewpoint held by most leading atheists today, and is often combined with the "Big Bang" theory.

The Big Bang theory proposes that the universe began with a very small and extremely dense compaction of matter and energy called the "Point of Singularity", which exploded to form our universe. Most atheists contend that the Point of Singularity came suddenly from complete nothingness. However, the Big Bang theory itself does not postulate the origin of the Point of Singularity, and many Big Bang proponents do believe in God as the ultimate source.

> "It is beyond the realm of the Big Bang Model to say what gave rise to the Big Bang. There are a number of speculative theories about this topic, but none of them make realistically testable predictions as of yet." (NASA article "Foundations of Big Bang Cosmology")[8]

We can examine the theory that the universe came from complete nothingness both physically and logically. The major points are highlighted in the following diagram:

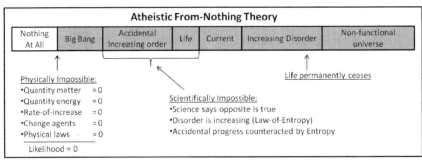

Figure 5

A) *Something-from-nothing*

Physically speaking, the universe coming from absolutely nothing is impossible according to the laws of science. The First Law of Thermodynamics states that the amount of energy in the universe is always constant; no new energy can come into existence. This is not a trivial technicality, but a fundamental law of the physical universe. <u>A logical corollary to the "first law" is that, in natural terms, there was not a point in time when energy came from nothing</u>. That would be an event in contradiction with known physical limitations.

The concept of something-from-nothing also contradicts everything we know of physical objects and processes – you cannot start with absolutely nothing and end up with something physical. Natural processes describe a transformation of something material into a different form – it would be completely foreign and unnatural for something physical to come into being from absolutely nothing. That would be the complete opposite of what we describe as a "natural" occurrence.

Logically speaking, the concept of something-from-nothing is impossible. A condition of complete nothingness and a universe with space, physical matter, and energy are by their very definition and nature mutually exclusive. There is no logical way to get from nothing to a physical universe, and "common sense" makes this very clear to anyone. It is important to note that the first state (nothingness) wouldn't actually even exist – nothing would! <u>"Where" and "what" would the universe be transitioning from, and what would the building blocks be? The answers are "nothing", "nothing", and "nothing"</u>. Within the confines of materialism and the absence of anything eternal or supernatural, common sense renders this logically impossible.

Quantitatively speaking, there is quite literally "nothing" to work with. In a condition of complete nothingness it is obvious that the quantity of all matter and energy would be zero, and also that the rate-of-increase and rate-of-change would be zero. No forces, processes, or laws would exist as agents of change. <u>Therefore, the increase of physical quantity would always equal zero, and the statistical likelihood of ever having anything physical would be zero. There is literally nothing that would ever cause this situation to change.</u> There would also be no place or space for anything to occur.

If space, energy, and matter appeared, then something exists that caused this to happen. Moreover, if something caused it to happen, then there was not actually a state of nothingness. If nothing existed 14 billion years ago, then nothing would exist now. Therefore, since the universe does indeed exist today, it is not true that there was nothingness at any time in the past. The temporal theory cannot be true.

Theories which propose longer and longer time frames (billions and trillions of years) for physical processes do not affect these conclusions. Those are still finite time frames that just leave atheism with the same impossibilities. The point is not how many millions or billions of years, but the distinction between finite time and infinite time. The infinite past is where the materialistic theories make no sense.

There is not, and never can be, a rational explanation of how the universe could come from complete nothingness. In my opinion, adherence to this theory requires a blind faith in the absence of any solid explanation.

B) Atheistic Theories Self-contradicting about Something-from-nothing

Because of these obvious problems with something-from-nothing, atheistic and agnostic authors sometimes say the universe came from nothing, but then imply that there was actually something pre-existing that enabled it to come from nothing. Stephen Hawking says, *"...the beginning of the universe was governed by the laws of science and doesn't need to be set in motion by some god".*[9] However, if there were any energy sources, laws, or space that were pre-existing, then it wasn't actually complete nothingness. As physicist Lawrence Krauss is quoted in USA Today:

> *"A physicist's version of nothing is very different from what we once thought it was."*
> (Dan Vergano quoting Lawrence Krauss)[10]

These statements reveal that leading proponents do not actually believe it is possible to get something from completely nothing. Since atheistic attempts at a rational explanation always begin with something, this in itself contradicts the concept of something-from-nothing. <u>This implicit acknowledgment by atheists and agnostics that the universe really could not have come from nothing is a foundational principle for the next chapters on the existence of God.</u>

The logical conclusion is that it is impossible for the physical universe to have come from nothing; at least, not without any supernatural help. From an atheistic perspective, there could not have been a point in time when this happened.

An atheist might then respond, "yes, this was not a natural occurrence, but an event superior to natural limitations". I agree with that logical conclusion, and it is one of the fundamental concepts of the next two chapters. <u>Physical principles tell us that the beginning of the universe was a "supernatural" event.</u>

C) Progression to Order and Life

Let us also consider the hopeful progression that is assumed to have occurred after the impossible something-from-nothing event. This is illustrated by the following diagram:

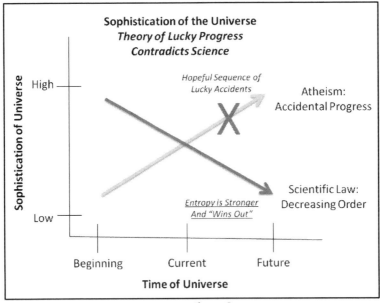

Figure 6

<u>Atheism is built upon a hypothetical sequence of lucky accidents over billions of years which eventually resulted in life on our planet.</u> This is shown in the diagram as the upward-sloping line.

However, the Second Law of Thermodynamics tells us that order is constantly decreasing (the term "entropy" is used for increasing disorder). This means that any accidental positive progress would have been quickly overcome by the large negative effects of entropy. The downward-sloping line illustrates this decreasing sophistication over time.

The very low probability of positive accidents is no match for the continual march of entropy, reversing any hypothetical positive steps. The law of entropy tells us that disorder "wins out", and the course is downward, away from sophistication and toward non-functional disorder. Therefore, no sustained positive progress would have been possible.

In this aspect, time is not the friend of atheistic theories. The more time, the more certain that any positive accidents would be wiped out by entropy. <u>Therefore, the notion of billions of years of positive progress resulting in life is in direct contradiction with the law of entropy.</u>

There is a contradiction when leading atheists acknowledge that the universe is running down (which is based on science), but claim that the universe increased in order for billions of years (which is based on hope/desire).

Order does not happen by accident, but is always the result of intelligent action, as we will discuss in the next chapter.

2. The Atheistic Eternal Option: Has the universe always existed?

The only other atheistic alternative is that everything physical has always existed, with no beginning and no supernatural help. However, most leading atheists today do not believe that it is possible that the universe has existed forever. Examples of this approach are Cyclic models (such as the Big Bounce theory) and the Steady State theory, which are actually in direct contradiction with each other.

Physically speaking, this alternative is also impossible. The law of entropy, mentioned above, tells us that disorder is constantly increasing. This law is a fundamental principle of the physical universe. A constant rate of decay clearly means that everything material will eventually be in a state of complete, nonfunctional disorder. If this process of decay started an infinite number of years ago, then it obviously would have already happened; complete disorder would have been accomplished a very long time ago!

Put another way, <u>any physical system that is still ordered could not have existed forever</u>. Since we live in a universe that has order, this universe could not have existed forever. Physically speaking, this would mean a direct contradiction of the law of entropy.

We could also consider this in terms of energy expenditure. Anything that is operating or functioning uses energy, and gradually runs down to a state of low-form energy. Viewing the universe as a whole, it started with a certain amount of energy, it uses energy to function, and it will eventually run-down to a condition of low-form energy which is non-functional and incapable of supporting life. Starting with any amount of useful energy, it will be "used up" after a finite amount of time. Therefore, <u>anything still operating (such as our entire universe) could not have existed for an infinite amount of time.</u>

In fact, it should be obvious from this discussion that the nature of our universe is completely inconsistent with the nature of an infinite amount of time. Our universe is obviously temporal in nature, since there is a rate of decay/entropy. We know that its existence is only for a finite amount of time; therefore, it was brought into existence at some time in the finite past.

There are various attempts by atheistic proponents to blur the finite nature of the universe through theories which hypothesize even larger amounts of matter and energy (such as multiple physical universes and huge energy sources). However, a larger amount of matter is still finite, and would have still gone to complete disorder in a finite amount of time. Regardless of the quantity of matter and energy, it is impossible for it to have existed forever. I am treating all physical matter and energy that has ever existed as one package, since we are looking at eternity-past and at the ultimate beginning in time of anything and everything that is physical.

Conclusions

Atheism is logically and physically impossible. As discussed in the sections above, today's physical universe could not have existed forever, and it is impossible for it to have come into existence from nothing. <u>There must be something that "connects" the physical universe with eternity-past, because it is incapable of standing on its own.</u> There is something that is the ultimate source, a foundation which does indeed extend through eternity-past.

The very concept of eternity-past (unlimited and infinite) is inconsistent with what we know of the physical and the natural (limited and finite). However, we know that there is an eternity-past, since something could not have come from nothing. This certainly goes far beyond the physical laws that we know, which means that the physical is not sufficient by itself. Eternity-past emphatically demonstrates that there is something superior to the physical, and demands that proper explanations will only come from discovering this "ultimate source".

Chapter 3
A Rational Explanation for the Universe

***There is an eternal ultimate source,
With specific attributes.***

*"Any skeptic worthy of the name
is both hunter and detective, stalking the evidence...
Skeptics are passionate about finding truth out"*
Mark Buchanan[11]

The overview in the previous chapter of the two atheistic options for the universe highlights the problems with materialism, but also begins to point us toward the truth. The two atheistic options ("Temporal" and "Eternal") contradict each other. Some atheists say that the universe could not have existed forever; therefore, it came from nothing at a specific point in time. Other atheists say that it could not have come from nothing; therefore, it has existed forever.

Each of these options has a part of the truth, which helps us further our inquiry into ultimate origins: (1) The universe started at a point in time, but this could not have been from complete nothingness, and (2) There is something that is eternal, but which is not subject to the law of increasing disorder.

Even though I have contended that it is physically and logically impossible that the universe could come from nothing, I do understand that someone can still choose to believe that it happened. Such a decision involves faith and the will.

However, I think that faith is best when accompanied by a reasonable explanation, and I ask you to search for a rational explanation that makes sense. A blind faith that it just happened without any sensible explanation is not sufficient. <u>However, if the fundamental assumption is that the universe actually came from nothing, then I don't believe there can ever be a rational description; the explanation is going to be "nothing", just like the hypothetical starting point.</u>

Based on our discussion so far, an atheist might say, "Okay, I agree that it is not rational for something to pop out of complete nothingness. Nevertheless, we don't need God. There is something else that is the ultimate source; a cosmic factory that produced the energy, matter, laws, and sophisticated order". I think that this rationale is implicit in the theories that we see from leading atheists. They don't really seem to believe the universe came from absolutely nothing, even though they won't say this directly. Their attempts at a rational explanation always imply that there is some pre-existing framework or factory that produces the building blocks.

In fact, beginning from a materialistic viewpoint, and based on our discussion from the last chapter, an <u>atheist seeking to form a rational framework as an alternative to God could come to the following series of fundamental principles for the ultimate source.</u>

This logical sequence starts with the following observation:

> Observation: *The universe exists, is sophisticated, and is running down*.

The universe began at a point in time

Most atheists agree that the universe could not have existed forever, because of the constant rate of increasing disorder and movement toward lower, non-functional energy. They believe there was a specific time in the past when it started, and that it had a high amount of energy. Since it will run down to non-functional disorder after a limited amount of time, but it is still functional now, it started a finite number of years ago.

The event that started the universe was radically non-natural

"Naturally" speaking, something physical cannot come from nothing. There must have been a "supernatural" (superior to the natural) event that caused physical matter and energy to come into existence. For example, the creation of the point-of-singularity (dense compaction of matter and energy) would have been needed prior to the Big Bang. This would not have been a natural occurrence, but an event that was creative and superior to natural limitations.

Suggestions of pre-existing energy sources and particle generators do not change the issue. Those would still be physical entities that could not have come from nothing, and eventually run down over time. We are talking about the origin of everything physical.

There was never complete nothingness

Since it is logically impossible for something to come from complete nothingness, but there is something today (the universe), then there never was a condition of nothingness; otherwise, nothing would ever exist. So there has been an infinite amount of absolute time in the past of existence, which we are calling eternity-past. There was never a time at which there was complete nothingness.

Something has always existed

Even leading atheistic theories rely on some pre-existing entity that is able to produce matter and energy. Therefore, something has existed forever, with no beginning point. Otherwise, nothing would exist now. This entity is "self-existent" (not created, but always existing), and the "ultimate source" of the universe.

The Ultimate Source has a nature superior to the physical

The entity which has existed forever is not subject to increasing disorder or reduction in energy, since it has maintained its functional abilities for an infinite amount of time. Also, it is capable of bringing the physical universe into existence. All known and hypothetical physical sources are subject to physical limitations and so do not qualify as the ultimate eternal source.

The Rational Explanation

This logical progression started from the observation that <u>the universe exists, is sophisticated, and is running down</u>. The striking but rational conclusion is that <u>there is an unseen, supernatural, eternal entity that created the universe</u>.

An atheist could reasonably determine the above principles and then state, "See, I have been able to describe a cosmic factory which is a rational basis for the origin of the universe, without need for a God."

But as a Christian I would say, "I agree that this is rational, but are you saying that your ultimate source is eternal, incorruptible, supernatural, and able to create the physical? I think that this is an excellent description of some of the fundamental attributes of God!"

And One More... High Order means the Ultimate Source is Intelligent

In addition to the above principles which might be deduced by an atheist, I believe that there is one more important and necessary attribute of the ultimate source: He is highly intelligent. As the below diagram illustrates, we can determine this because the universe was made with high order.

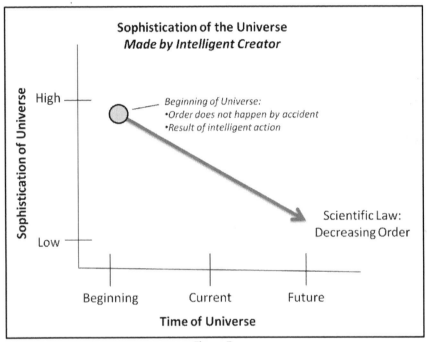

Figure 7

We know from observation and science that the universe is sophisticated right now ("Current" time in the diagram), and that the universe has increasing disorder (downward slope of sophistication). Therefore, looking backward, we know that it actually started with a high degree of order initially ("Beginning" time in the diagram), from which it has been decreasing.

Sophisticated order does not happen by accident, but is always the result of intelligent action. Animals create nests, people create houses, and something created a highly-ordered and sophisticated universe capable of supporting life. So the ultimate source which made the universe is extremely intelligent.

Intelligence is the attribute of the ultimate source which is most often avoided by atheistic theories, since it points directly to God, especially when combined with the other supernatural attributes from above. The next chapter will directly examine the existence of God as well as His attributes which can be determined from science and reason.

The Two Realities

Our journey has now taken us to the place where we can logically understand that there are actually two realities, as shown in the diagram below.

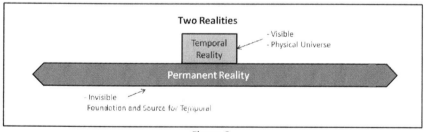

Figure 8

The reality in which we live and which we can directly observe is temporary. There is another reality which has existed forever and will always exist into the future. Even though we are not able to see it with our eyes at this time, we are able to understand some of its properties. Moreover, it is the foundation and source for our own temporary universe. What we see is the small melting tip of the iceberg which we do not see. And the unseen part of the iceberg is made of something far more permanent, which does not melt!

We are sadly mistaken if we believe that the universe is the only true reality, and anything else is mythical and religious. The foundational reality is much more concrete and permanent than our universe, and it is worthwhile to apply our minds and imaginations to continue the exploration of eternity past and future.

Scientific exploration sometimes takes us to the "edge" of the physical universe, but rarely attempts to carry us over to what is beyond the edge. There was a point in time at which a supernatural event occurred, when the permanent reality brought the temporal reality into existence.

Chapter 4
God and Eternity-Past

***The existence of a Supernatural Creator
is logically and physically necessary.
Several of His attributes can be determined.***

"It is fatal to let people suppose that Christianity is only a mode of feeling; it is vitally necessary to insist that it is first and foremost a rational explanation of the universe."
Dorothy Sayers

A look at eternity-past shows the impossibility of materialism (the theory that only matter and energy exist, and that nothing beyond these has ever existed). Today's physical universe could not have existed forever, and it is impossible for it to have come into existence from nothing.

Scientific views which start at a finite point in the past should be expanded to facilitate consideration of the true source of our temporal universe. Even a time frame of billions of years (used so often today to signify an enormous time frame sufficient for anything) is very small in comparison to eternity. The more that we stare into eternity, ponder ever-increasing time frames, and then consider time with no beginning, the smaller the time frame of the universe appears. No matter how long ago we postulate for the beginning of the universe, the length of time before that was still infinite.

There is an enormous difference between a scientific view that focuses solely on the temporal, and a scientific view that looks directly into the eternal and the infinite. The conclusions of the first will be minor, and the conclusions of the second will be of eternal significance. I encourage you to enthusiastically consider a rational explanation of eternity-past and the origin of the universe.

Identifying God as the Ultimate Source

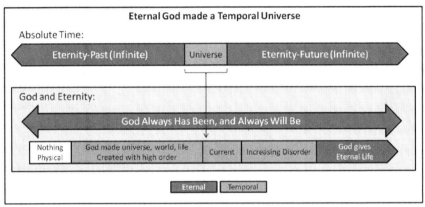

Figure 9

Our discussion of atheism (Chapter 2) led us to the conclusion that there is something superior to matter and energy. Next, our search for a rational explanation (Chapter 3) established a series of logical principles about the ultimate source of the universe. We arrived at these principles through observation, science, and reason. These are not "religious" truths, but are rational and scientific.

We can now apply what we have learned directly to a rational discussion of the existence of God. He is the ultimate source who created the sophisticated physical universe from nothing physical. However, we do not want to leave this as a simplistic identification, nor do we need to. We will now seek to further understand His nature.

The Necessary Attributes of God

It is striking to see that we can go much further than establishing the existence of God. There are actually several important facts about the nature of God which can be deduced. These are not based on the Bible or hopeful invention, but on the rational principles which were established in Chapter 3.

The following diagram summarizes the attributes of God that can be deduced from science and logic:

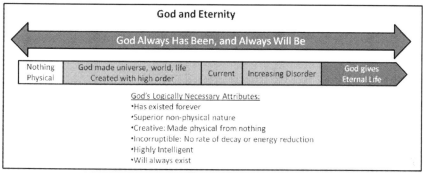

Figure 10

1) God has existed forever, from eternity-past.

There is something/someone that is eternal. We know this because it is not possible for something (whether natural or supernatural) to originate from complete nothingness. God, as the ultimate source of everything, could not have begun at a point in time. It is necessary for something to be eternal, so He has existed from eternity-past. He never had a "beginning", and did not even create Himself.

Sometimes atheists will say that having a God doesn't solve anything, because "Who made God?". However, we do not believe that God was ever created, but that He has always existed. As established in Chapter 3, the ultimate source has always existed, being "self-existent". This is the only possibility that makes sense and allows for a rational explanation.

Therefore, God existed for an infinite time before the creation of the physical universe.

2) God does not have a physical nature, because matter and energy could not have existed forever, as discussed in chapter 2. He is "supernatural"– His nature surpasses physical restrictions and is infinitely superior to matter, energy, and physical laws.

3) He can create the physical out of nothing, which is "naturally" impossible. God is able to bring matter and energy into existence without any pre-existing foundational resources. He creates and supplies the building blocks of space, operational time, physical matter, energy, and laws. He is able to surpass the physical laws and restrictions to create something physical from nothing physical.

4) God is incorruptible. He has no entropy, no rate-of-decay, no reduction of energy. We know this, because any rate of reduction would have brought Him to complete non-functional disorder after a finite amount of time.

Since the physical universe has existed for a finite amount of time, we know that He created the universe a finite number of years in the past. He existed an infinite amount of time before that without reduction to disorder. Therefore, we know that He has a "zero" rate of decay, of increasing entropy, and of reduction of energy.

In fact, He also has a zero risk-level or failure-factor, since an infinite amount of time would have caused even a very low-percentage risk to have occurred, with 100% probability.

God's incorruptible nature is the opposite of the physical nature. Because of entropy, we know from the previous chapter that the physical universe is temporal and could not have existed forever. Consequently, because we know God has existed forever, then we also know that He has no entropy and no faults.

5) God is Intelligent: The law of entropy tells us that the universe is steadily moving toward nonfunctional disorder. Therefore, it was created in a highly ordered and functional condition, even greater than what we observe today. The sophisticated design and utility for life was original, established by someone with an intellect far superior to our own.

The following diagram illustrates why we know God is highly intelligent. This was explained in Chapter 3.

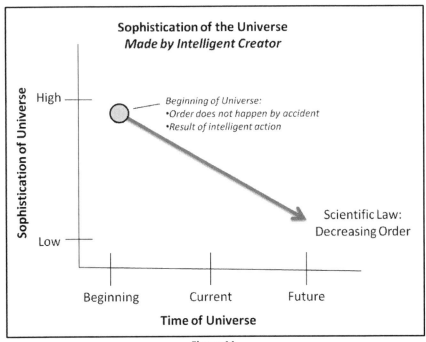

Figure 11

Order does not happen by accident, but is always the result of intelligent action. Animals create nests, people create houses, and God created a highly-ordered and sophisticated universe.

As mentioned before, there is a contradiction when leading atheists acknowledge that the universe is running down, but claim that the universe increased in order for billions of years. Any order at the beginning would have come from an intelligent creator. If there was a Big Bang, the explosion itself could not have produced order. We know from experience that explosions do the opposite of this!

6) Eternity-future: Since God is eternal, and has no decay or entropy, He will always exist, into the infinite future. This will

become a foundation for looking into eternity-future in upcoming chapters.

In summary, God is infinite and unlimited, perfect and incorruptible, and able to bring the physical out of nothing. He has always existed, and will exist into the future.

Chapter 5
Intentional Evidence

God purposely provided us with proof that He exists.

God has provided a means by which we can know that He does exist based on an examination of our world in terms of eternity-past. Although we are not yet treating the Bible as a source of truth, it is useful to look at a passage which claims that this method was intentionally provided by God:

> ... that which is known about God is evident within them; for <u>God made it evident to them</u>. For since the creation of the world <u>His invisible attributes</u>, <u>His eternal power</u> and <u>divine nature</u>, have been <u>clearly seen</u>, being understood through what has been made, so that they are without excuse. (Romans 1:19-20)

This passage states that critical truths about God can be understood through what has been created, and that He has made it evident to us. <u>This indicates a clear purpose by God to give us actual evidence</u>, and not just to ask for blind faith. He has given us the ability to understand and deduce important concepts about Himself from the world. This passage states that although these things are "invisible", they are also "clearly seen", "understood", and sufficient for everyone to believe in God. This is an important aspect of faith: with our minds, seeing (thinking and knowing) things that are not visible.

There is a sense in which this passage refers to temporal aspects (e.g., since the world is beautiful and has objects that were obviously designed, then we know that God exists). However, it actually means much more in regard to eternity-past, especially since it specifically mentions God's "eternal power". The existence of the physical universe with its very important laws allows us to clearly deduce that there is a God, and (as this passage states) that He is "eternal", has a "divine nature", and has other specific "invisible attributes".

These supernatural attributes can seem unreal, but they are logically necessary. We know the "physical nature", and understand that it is temporal. There is also a "divine nature" that has these attributes. The divine nature is perfect and pure, eternal and creative. The physical nature is a creation of the divine, an excellent nature but with limitations and imperfections.

Conclusions about the Existence of God

Leading atheists say that they are looking for the single unifying theory for our physical universe. I believe that the most fundamental and important component is: "God has always existed". This provides the foundation for ultimate origin in a way that makes sense with eternity-past, and also gives order, meaning, and purpose to our universe.

Thee very first sentence of the Bible claims: *"In the beginning God created the heavens and the earth." (Genesis 1:1).* This is a statement of something eternal creating the material, saying that at a specific point in time, God made the physical come into existence. Some people would call this a "religious" statement, but I believe it is actually an important statement regarding the history of the universe, and is the basis for a single unifying theory.

The atheistic world-view has persisted partly because of a neglect of the consideration of eternal things. Most discussions of origins focus on small and recent questions, but eternity-past is the bigger question with larger and more significant conclusions. Specifically, as we have demonstrated, a consideration of eternity-past provides a basis for understanding the existence of God and His divine attributes.

These infinite truths are sometimes difficult for our finite minds to grasp. We do not understand eternity, although we can define and discuss it. We do not comprehend completely the nature of an infinite God, but we know that He is necessary, and that He does exist. There is temptation to think that since we cannot see God, He does not exist. However, our reasoning clearly tells us that He is more real and permanent than the physical things we see.

These are not just concepts or illusions. There is an eternity-past, God does exist, and He is an eternal being, incorruptible, the author of physical life, and (as we shall consider in subsequent chapters) the giver of eternal life.

Fortunately we can <u>leave behind the empty atheistic perspective of "from nothing to nothing", and embrace "from eternity-past to eternity-future"</u> with an infinite God and creator. From an ambiguous and relative system of knowledge, we can move to infinite truth and certainty. What the atheist thought was truth (materialism) is actually impossible, and what was considered impossible (God) is a necessary and foundational truth. The notion that belief in God is based on unreal illusions is false. It is grounded in the most fundamental science, and in permanent truth.

And most important, what we have learned from eternity-past gives us a foundation to consider eternity-future. God will always exist, into eternity-future, and He also has total command of the physical. He is able to do with the physical what is naturally impossible (such as creating something from nothing). This gives us hope of eternal life, since He holds both eternity and the physical firmly in His hand.

Part 2: Infinite Value

Chapter 6
Philosophies that Ignore Eternity

An obsessive focus on the here-and-now causes many people to base all truth on today's temporary physical life, and suppresses the desire to understand eternity.
Ignoring eternity is illogical and extremely dangerous.

"Truth is always <u>about</u> something,
but reality is that <u>about which</u> truth is."
C.S. Lewis

The term "Secular" is often used to refer to non-religious activities or institutions. It means the current, temporal world, with all of its attributes, objects, and activities. This concept is useful because, of course, we all live and function in the here-and-now.

However, we live in an age in which many leading intellectuals have made the secular perspective a worldview, and even developed it into a belief system. "Secularism" is a term used to indicate an extreme secular focus which is comparable to a religion. All truth, values, and decisions are based on "the now", and there is an intense resistance to being influenced by anything from eternity-past or eternity-future.

This view is dominant in many aspects of society today, although most of its adherents do not even directly realize they are living by such a philosophy. Many proponents in the media and in education are, in my opinion, purposely suppressing the discussion of eternity, stressing that "there is no tomorrow – only today". They either deny that eternity exists or imply that it is beyond knowing and consequently should be ignored. Because of both what is rejected (eternity) and what is embraced (the here-and-now), the resulting knowledge and values are relative, based on experience, and purposely changing with the times.

Many intellectuals have developed philosophies about how to live in a world without eternity, without God, and without absolutes. In order to avoid a lack of purpose, they have tried to obtain meaning where no meaning exists, and hope where no hope exists. Some of these worldviews are thousands of years old, and others originated within the last couple of centuries. Many of these are similar to each other, but emphasize different aspects.

I will briefly discuss four of these philosophies: Existentialism, Secular Humanism, Hedonism, and Nihilism. I am only referring to the atheistic versions of these theories. We will then look at why I claim that these philosophies are "Illogical and Extremely Dangerous".

Existentialism: Meaning is through Individual Experience

Existentialism has had an immense impact upon today's societies. The foundational tenet is that there is no absolute meaning or purpose in the universe, but each person creates his own relative meaning through individual experiences and expression.

Therefore, truth is regarded as: "You believe what is right for you, and it is true for you. I believe what is right for me, and it is true for me." It is not necessary for an individual's beliefs to match up with an absolute reality, as long as they are useful for personal feelings and happiness.

In this philosophy, truth is subjective, relative, and individual. Moreover, the concept of truth is not very important; only the individual experience really matters.

Secular Humanism: Truth is created by the Society

Secular Humanism is similar to Existentialism, although there is more of an emphasis on humanity as a whole (Society) rather than on the individual. There are no absolutes, but truth and values are created, molded, and continually changed by the society. Man is the norm by which values are to be determined; he is autonomous.

You can see the effects and teachings of Secular Humanism on our own societies today. They proclaim that they have created a "better morality" than any previous God-based system. In a sense, when it comes to truth and values, they have created their own humanistic religion.

The Illusion of Meaning and Truth

When viewed from an eternal perspective, atheistic Existentialism and Humanism are representative of a vain attempt to say: "We came from nothing, and will go to nothing, but in between there is high dignity and meaning." However, it doesn't make sense to imply high value in a context of complete emptiness, and I think it is just a cover for what is really a lack of meaning and no hope for the future. Good or bad actions really have no consequence for better or worse, for each individual will soon cease to exist, and this will be followed ultimately by the elimination of society as a whole.

Relative truth ultimately means there really is no truth at all. People following these philosophies (whether by name or not) are travelling down a road that leads both everywhere and nowhere, since it is subject to individual decisions and experiences. Most importantly, if the end result for each person will be ceasing to exist in a few years, then <u>the road actually leads to a cliff with nothing but emptiness beyond</u>.

Hedonism: Purpose is Pleasure

The philosophy of Hedonism is pleasure-seeking taken to an extreme. Certainly it is very good for all of us to enjoy life and to avoid pain, but in Hedonism the pursuit of pleasure actually becomes the most important purpose of life.

This view is another logical consequence of a rejection of eternal life, but in this case one decides to "have as much fun as possible" rather than "create as much meaning as possible". Many people have adopted this worldview as a way of life and overall purpose without specifically understanding or choosing Hedonism.

As with Existentialism, the Hedonist philosophy becomes similar to a religion. It implies both a truth system and a value system:
- Truth: The principle for determining True-or-False is based on usefulness for the lifestyle, especially in regard to whether an activity causes pleasure or pain;
- Values: The moral judgment of Good-versus-Bad is directly based on increasing pleasure versus hindering pleasure

The ultimate good and purpose in Hedonism is pleasure: "If it feels good, then do it, because it is right!". We obviously see this in wide practice today. People's feelings are turned into a moral purpose, with the principle that "pleasure is right".

Both the Existentialist and the Hedonist want to promote and protect indulgence in various activities, but for slightly different reasons – one for the experiential meaning, the other for the pleasure.

It is interesting that you could go to most large universities today and clearly see all three of these major secular philosophies being actively pursued. You can see two of them in some of the classrooms (professors teaching their students in Humanism/Existentialism), and the other in the dormitories and fraternities (many of these same students actively practicing Hedonism). Both groups are at least ignoring, and possibly rejecting, both God and eternity. In some ways, they are spinning in a temporary whirlpool without considering what lies beyond.

Nihilism: No meaning or hope

Another philosophy which is a consequence of the atheistic worldview is called "Nihilism". The Latin word "nihil" literally means "nothing". This philosophy holds that since we came from nothing and have a very limited future, then there really is no objective meaning, purpose, or value to the universe or our individual lives. Unfortunately, adherents of this view often descend into deep despair.

Illogical and Extremely Dangerous

It is amazing that so many of today's philosophers and scientists consider it counter-productive to consider the whole breadth of eternity and to attempt to look into the deep past or the distant future. They are so focused on the temporal that they refuse to think of eternity and God, and end up actually cutting out some large and important aspects of science and the physical universe.

I believe that a decision to ignore eternity is illogical and dangerous, because of the comparative value of eternal life and the fact that not looking for eternal truth probably means you won't find it. Rather than just assuming that there is not an eternity-future or that we cannot influence it, we should seek diligently to determine whether that truly is the case. Someone who has not studied eternity-past and eternity-future should not claim that such knowledge is unattainable.

It is illogical to assert that a relative and temporal approach to truth will lead a person to sufficient conclusions of absolute and permanent truth (a fallacy of relevance, in which the premises and inferences are not adequate for the conclusions). In fact, such an approach will actually prevent the obtaining of permanent truth since it excludes the necessary components. In addition, implying that truth about eternity-future is just relative according to individual opinion is a subjectivist fallacy (treating an objective conclusion as subjective).

Only a willingness to examine eternity will lead us to reasonable conclusions on which to base our beliefs and actions. Similar to the truism that someone without goals will reach them (since they will accomplish no goals), someone who does not seek eternal truth will probably find exactly what they are searching for. If there is a way to influence our eternity but we do not find it, then we have committed a mistake with catastrophic results and the loss of an enormous opportunity. The cost of looking for permanent truth is minimal, but the risk of not looking is very high indeed.

Conclusions

In the midst of these philosophical efforts to bring purpose to a temporary age, it should be obvious that the concept of a future eternal life with love, beauty, and pleasure is infinitely more superior and desirable; consequently, it is certainly worth the time and effort to search whether it is possible.

If you are an adherent to any of these philosophies, I ask you to not let an obsessive focus on the here-and-now crowd out your willingness to consider eternal things. Your potential for understanding permanent truth has perhaps been limited by a total focus on the temporal. I encourage you to use your mind to start thinking out-of-the-box, about the eternal. I even ask you to use your imagination; not to think about unreal things, but to consider what is real and permanent.

I ask you to consider that eternity is not something unreal, but is very real indeed. I believe you will find that it is actually very exciting and intellectually stimulating to apply your mind to explore infinite time frames. Coming up in the next section will be consideration of a knowledge-based approach for discovering truth about eternity-future.

Chapter 7
The Infinite Value of Eternal Life

We should actively investigate whether eternal life is possible.

"In Your presence is fullness of joy;
In Your right hand there are pleasures forever"
Psalm 16:11

Understanding Eternity-Future

Most of us are interested in knowing more about our ultimate destiny. We would like to know the truth about the fate of our universe, our planet and, of course, our own individual existence. However, you might think that obtaining truth about the distant future is not possible, and that you could have little influence over your own destiny anyway.

I believe that knowledge of eternity-future is both attainable and worthwhile, and we will discuss a logical method for investigating the future and exploring whether it is possible to obtain eternal life. I realize that you are not interested in illusions that give false hope, but that you want to know the truth, and you require both evidence and sound reasoning regarding such important matters.

Knowledge of the Eternal Future is Intellectually Attainable

A common assumption by both atheists and agnostics is that eternity-future is beyond knowing; that there is no scientific or intelligent way to obtain truth about such things. They believe that those who claim to know about eternal matters are simply placing blind faith in a set of fanciful concepts which were created by men.

As discussed in Part 1, scientific views are adequate only if they encompass infinite time frames. When these views are enhanced to consider eternity-past I believe they lead to specific strong and reasonable conclusions regarding the existence and character of God.

But then a transition needs to be made from a discussion of God's existence to specific knowledge about eternity-future. I think that this transition is often neglected in presentations of evidence for God, and assumptions are made which might not be in alignment with the reader's methods of knowing.

I have attempted to lay out the details of an appropriate transition throughout the next chapters, in a manner that proceeds logically from the existence of God to knowledge regarding eternity-future and eternal life. Rather than a leap of faith, I intend to present a method of knowing in which you can discover verifiable evidence of supernatural revelation, and then progress to a knowledge-based faith in eternity-future.

Faith for the future does not need to be a blind trust in invented hope, but can be a knowledge based decision to rely on critical truths from a verifiable source of supernatural revelation. Such faith involves the imagination to enable your mind to go beyond the current temporal realities to comprehend invisible and infinite truths regarding eternal time frames.

As an example of faith, suppose that an engineer from a developed country visits an isolated jungle tribe and describes unseen technological products such as cell phones, cars, and airplanes. Some people from the tribe might immediately believe the engineer, but others might demand more proof. They might demand a systematic way of knowing which requires evidence that the engineer can be trusted and that the technologies are based upon firm science. Subsequent affirmation by these people will then be based on knowledge, but will also require faith and imagination. Faith does not mean that the technologies are not real, simply that they are not directly seen and physically accessible.

Knowledge about the Eternal Future is Worthwhile

Many people have chosen to ignore the prospect of life-after-death, and perhaps consider eternal life to be undesirable and not worthy of intellectual attention. However, I ask you to take a brief look at both death and eternity-future and to consider whether there is value in an exploration of these matters. <u>I do not mean to imply that the desire for eternal life proves that it is true, but that the desire should motivate you to diligently search for the truth.</u> We will then consider evidence and reasoning for eternal truth.

1) Do we cease to exist after death?

It is clear that most people desire to avoid death for as long as possible, and would prolong its coming perpetually if they could. Dying is greatly feared, and ceasing to exist forever is infinitely worse. At the personal level, this would literally mean entering "nothingness". Some atheists acknowledge the dreary consequences of this approach:

> *"Not only are you bound to die and leave this world; you are bound to leave it in* such *precipitate fashion that the present significance of anything—your relationships, your plans for the future, your hobbies, your possessions—will appear to have been totally illusory." (Sam Harris, The End of Faith)*[12]

We have all observed the intense ongoing efforts to live longer, both by individual measures such as healthy eating and exercise, and by the medical community's efforts to cure and prevent diseases. This is, of course, an effort driven by the desire to live as long as possible, and to delay the time when we might cease to exist. However, these health and medical measures cannot prolong death by very long – perhaps by a few decades at most. We all know that there are limits to any natural extensions of life, and prolonging one's temporal existence to one hundred years or so still leaves it finite. Natural life as we know it is always finite.

There has also been a renewed interest in the theory of reincarnation, which is the teaching of some Eastern religions that the end of a person's physical life is followed by the rebirth of that person's soul, in another type of physical body. For many people today, this is an attempt to have life-after-death without God. However, in a purely physical universe, this is of course an impossible scenario, since reincarnation would be dependent on spiritual and supernatural elements to be true.

Moreover, we obviously cannot consider "being remembered" or "leaving our mark" as an ongoing existence. Such may perhaps provide a little comfort to some before dying, but would not in any way cause one to be alive or conscious after death. As Woody Allen put it:

> *"I don't want to achieve immortality through my work; I want to achieve immortality through not dying."*
> (Woody Allen)[13]

The topic of life-after-death deserves a diligent search, but unfortunately many people assume that it is beyond knowing. Consequently, they do not apply their minds to investigate and search important questions such as:
- *When I die, will I totally cease to exist?*
- *Do I have a soul or spirit which is not physical and does not cease to exist at the point of death?*
- *Does my consciousness and some part of my mind continue on with this spirit, or are these only psychological aspects of my physical brain?*

Physically speaking, we know that the body and the brain cease to function upon death, and both start to decay immediately. So we know that the physical cannot go on, at least not naturally. There would need to be something "supernatural" in order for a person's physical body and brain to function again at some point in the future. A supernatural force or entity would be superior to the physical and not subject to its limitations.

If you do not have a spirit, and the physical gets no supernatural help, then you would totally and permanently cease to exist at the point of death. There would be no more physical life, and no more mental life: no thinking, no consciousness, no awareness. This is a logical consequence of atheism, and in the next chapter we will examine some philosophical attempts to divert attention away from any existence after death.

2) The infinite value of eternal life

Since living is probably something that you like to do, then living forever would be fantastic, and ceasing to live would be horrible. Quantitatively speaking, if each day of your life is valuable to you, then living forever is of infinite value. If you would be happy to know that you had one hundred years left to live, then you should be infinitely happy to know that you have eternity left to live.

I do realize that some people who are suffering greatly do not consider a day of life as a thing of value. However, for the sake of this discussion, and for the sake of understanding the ultimate value that might be possible with eternal life, I ask you to think in terms of a life in which each day is filled with love, beauty, and pleasure. The ultimate goal for eternity-future is infinite time, infinite love, infinite beauty, and infinite pleasure. This is obviously extremely desirable, and I also believe it is attainable. An explanation of the nature of eternal life is provided in a later chapter.

I think that when you truly consider the matter, you will enthusiastically agree that you want to live forever, and never cease to exist. Moreover, this desire should motivate you to search for it. The degree to which you want something should determine the degree to which you will search for it.

Motivation to investigate whether Eternal Life is possible

If you acknowledge the infinite value of living forever, then you should realize that it is worth your effort to at least search for truth. If you then decide that eternal life is not possible, you should turn your focus to lengthening the time of your temporary life and to enjoying temporal pleasures. However, if you decide that eternal life is at least possible, then I believe that you should focus your efforts on discovering how to obtain it.

Part 3: The Revelation of Truth

Chapter 8
Faith and Revelation

*Knowledge of eternity-future cannot be obtained by observation and deduction.
We should earnestly seek to know whether God has communicated eternal truth.*

We are stepping through a logical progression starting from eternity-past and ending with eternity-future. We have presented reasoning for the existence of God and deduced several of His divine attributes, including that He will exist forever. However, we are not yet at the point of looking directly at eternity-future and the destiny of the human race.

As we transition to learning about eternity-future, we will also transition to another method of discovering truth. Questions about eternity-future cannot be answered by physical means; this knowledge is beyond human reasoning and scientific discovery.

There is only one way that we can come to know the other eternal truths, <u>which is for God to tell us.</u> He is the One who has lived forever and created the physical universe. He will exist into eternity-future, has complete control over the physical, and probably has plans for the future. <u>We will only understand His plans if He has decided to communicate to us.</u> The diagram below illustrates this transition.

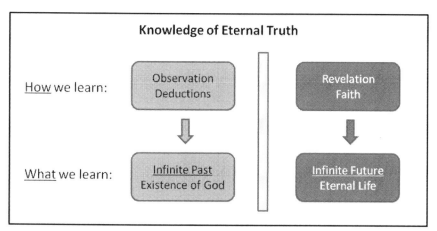

Figure 12

The first chapters on "The Existence of God" focused on the left side of the diagram. The next section on "The Infinite Value of Eternal Life" presented reasons why it is worthwhile to search for knowledge of the eternal future. We now move to the right side of the diagram, in which revelation and faith are needed in order to learn about the infinite future.

Even though we can determine that God exists, we do not see Him today, and most of us do not hear Him speaking audibly. However, communication from God is necessary for us to learn the most important truths. This chapter discusses some principles that are important for looking into revelation from God.

Revelation from a trusted source is an important method of learning for all of us. We count on textbooks, teachers, and news reporters to communicate knowledge which we cannot directly obtain otherwise. Most of what we know of world geography, history, and scientific principles was obtained through listening and reading.

This book contends that written revelation from God is the bridge to continuing on the path of knowledge about eternity. Through written form, if He so desired, God could communicate knowledge much more clearly and specifically than by other means. It would be consistent through the ages, and would be "verifiable".

We will soon look into the area of written revelation in detail. However, let's first examine how we come to know about things that are invisible.

Faith: Knowing things that are Unseen

Eternal things are invisible and not easily verified by normal scientific means. However, a logical analysis indicates that infinite things such as eternity-past and a supernatural God do exist and are actually fundamental to understanding the universe. So we can "know" these things, but in a different manner than we know the physical items in our day-to-day lives.

Much of scientific exploration requires the use of imagination to think about and discuss principles and objects that are unseen; for example, the discovery and modeling of molecules, atoms, and sub-atomic particles. Imagination is also important for an understanding of infinite and eternal truths. It is profitable to expand your science beyond the current temporal realm, and to involve your imagination to investigate invisible truths which are beyond the physical; otherwise, you will be limited in the reach of your scientific understanding.

If your science is in a limited box, then you will never be able to stare into eternity-past or eternity-future and answer the most important questions in life. For the critical and infinite questions, you will continue to come up with temporary physical answers.

After coming to a realization that there is indeed an infinite and eternal God, we can start to use our minds to think of eternity-future and the possibilities that lay ahead. We can look for an intelligent God who is the ultimate source of our universe, search for communication from Him, and seek to know the spiritual and eternal truths that God might have for us to discover.

Since we do not see God, and do not see eternity-past or eternity-future, <u>it is only by faith that we can know these truths.</u> Faith is concerned with affirming the knowledge of <u>actual truths</u> that are unseen. I am not talking about things that are fiction or fantasy, but about things that are real and true.

We are not yet treating the Bible as a source of truth, but it is useful to look at its description of faith.

The logic for the existence of God laid out in the first couple of chapters describes concepts which are unseen, and therefore require faith to be convinced of their truth. We don't see God, and we didn't see the universe created, but the following passage says we know by faith that these things are true:

> *<u>By faith we understand</u> that the worlds were prepared by the word of God, so that what is seen was <u>not made out of things which are visible</u>. (Hebrews 11:3)*

And more than just intellectual knowledge, the Bible describes <u>faith as the combination of being convinced of something unseen, and a decision to rely on that truth as something critical</u>:

> *Now faith is the assurance of [things] hoped for, the conviction of things not seen. (Hebrews 11:1).*

One aspect of faith is how we obtain knowledge, and the other aspect is trusting in something critical based on that knowledge. With regard to eternity-past, we emphasize that faith is necessary to understand ultimate origins. For eternity-future, faith in a reliable source of revelation enables us to acquire knowledge, but we each then decide how to utilize that knowledge and whether to personally trust in those truths.

We see a similar principle with wisdom: when we say that someone is wise, the first aspect is that he somehow gained wisdom, and the second aspect is that he makes decisions based on that special knowledge.

The Bible Claims to be God's Written Revelation

It is important to seek whether God has communicated to us. There are several books which claim to have been given by God, and we should look for evidence that would demonstrate supernatural revelation. I don't think the search should be viewed as, *"which religion is right?"*, but rather as, *"which written revelation, if any, was given by God?"*. For example, rather than looking at "Christianity" as commonly understood, it is much more useful to look at the Bible which has the Jewish and Christian scriptures.

This book contends that the Bible is God's written revelation to all people. Let's first look at the claims that the Bible makes about itself, and then in the next chapters we will look for evidence as to whether these claims are true.

<u>Prophets:</u> The Bible claims that God decided to speak through men who wrote down exactly what He wanted to communicate.

God communicated His eternal truths to the prophets, who spoke for God and wrote His truths in the Bible:

> *But know this first of all, that no prophecy of Scripture is [a matter] of one's own interpretation, for <u>no prophecy was ever made by an act of human will</u>, but <u>men moved by the Holy Spirit spoke from God</u>. (2 Peter 1:19-21)*

<u>Trustworthy Revelation:</u> The above passage claims that the true prophets of God were recording exactly what God was communicating through them. Moreover, it is asserted that these truths contain God's intentional instructions to be read, believed, and acted upon by all people. Following is a statement with more specifics on what the Bible claims to mean for each of us personally:

> *All Scripture is inspired by God and profitable for teaching, for reproof, for correction, for training in righteousness… (2 Timothy 3:16)*

These and other passages, if true, present some very important implications about the Bible. The word translated "inspired" means much more than a powerful influence. Literally, the word is "God breathed", which means that God caused the human authors to write exactly what He wanted.

<u>Eternity-future:</u> The most important instructions we should be looking for are those regarding eternity-future. Extremely important for our purposes, we see a bold claim by Paul, who wrote several sections of the Bible:

> *For I would have you know, brethren, that <u>the gospel</u> which was preached by me is not according to man. For I neither received it from man, nor was I taught it, but <u>[I received it] through a revelation of Jesus Christ.</u>*
> *(Galatians 1:11-12)*

The Bible here makes the very strong and exciting claim that the "gospel" (the good news about how to obtain eternal life) was given directly by God Himself and written in the Bible. If true, this is of course exactly what you should be looking for – not only the hope of eternal life, but actual direct communication by God on the specific criteria needed in order to live forever.

God Wants You to Seek Him

The Bible claims that God wants people to seek for His truths, to try to discover what He has communicated to us about Himself:

> *God has looked down from heaven upon the sons of men to see if there is anyone who understands, who seeks after God. (Psalm 53:2)*

As we now turn our thoughts to search for clears answers about eternity-future, we will obviously need to utilize faith in order to come to a knowledge regarding things that are yet to happen and promises about our own destiny:

> *And without faith it is impossible to please [Him], for he who comes to God must believe that He is and [that] He is a rewarder of those who seek Him. (Hebrews 11:6)*

This tells us that <u>God will reward you if you personally seek Him</u>. I ask you now to seek to determine whether He has communicated how to have eternal life, and then to have faith in what He communicates. *(Note: The word "believe" is just the verb form of "faith" – they have the same root meaning)*. He has promised that anyone who earnestly searches for God's truths will find them:

> *...those who diligently seek Me will find Me.*
> *(Proverbs 8:17)*

Therefore, in order to come to an understanding of eternity-future, you will need:
1. A decision to search for God's truth (*"He is a rewarder of those who seek Him"*, Hebrews 11:6);
2. A knowledge-based approach for discovering supernatural truths (chapters 9-10);
3. A personal decision to trust upon those truths if you discover them; to have faith regarding eternity-future

God has provided evidence on which to base our faith

God does not force anyone to believe, but in my opinion He has supplied sufficient evidence upon which we can confidently decide to place our faith. He has purposely given us verifiable evidence so that we would (1) Know that He exists, as described in chapter 4; and (2) Trust the Bible in regard to eternal life, as described next in chapters 9 and 10.

I believe that God has not been silent, because He has given us written revelation which is exactly what He wants us to know. He has chosen a written form of communication rather than directly being visible and speaking to us. This is intentional and requires us to expand our ways of knowing to have faith, in order to see what is unseen. This method enables us to search, to read the Bible, and to discover the critical truths about eternal life. In the next chapters we will explore whether the Bible is the book that is God's revelation of eternal truths.

Chapter 9
The Revelation of Truth

__Writings which provide verifiable proof of completely accurate supernatural revelation can be trusted for instruction in eternal life.__

I believe that God has chosen a written form of communication rather than directly being visible and speaking to us, and this written revelation describes exactly what He wants us to know regarding eternity-future. God could have done so without providing any supporting evidence. He could have just given us His Book, and decreed that we need to blindly believe statements which are unverifiable about the future and eternal-life. That is how a lot of people view faith in God today-a blind guess without any proof.

However, I am convinced that <u>God has intentionally provided us with proof on which to base our faith in the Bible</u>. This chapter and the subsequent chapter provide an overview and details of God's method for demonstrating the trustworthiness of His revelation. God does not force anyone to believe, but He has supplied sufficient evidence upon which we can confidently decide to place our faith. We will now look into the method He has provided to prove that the Bible can be trusted for knowledge about eternity-future.[14]

Evidence for the Written Revelation of Truth

If you believe that God exists, your next task is to seek to determine if He has provided a written form of communication. The main point of this chapter is to describe for you the manner and method that God has intentionally provided to give you sufficient evidence for the trustworthiness of the Bible.

The Bible describes how Jesus was telling His followers that He would soon be put to death on a cross, and would then be resurrected from the dead. He then told them:

> *Now I have told you before it happens, so that when it happens, you may believe. (John 14:29)*

This statement describes a general and important principle in the Bible: God telling people details of an event in advance, so that when it happened, they would believe in Him. These are specific prophecies that would require supernatural knowledge to predict the event, and sometimes also required a supernatural fulfillment. This method can be specified as follows:

1. Many times in the Bible, God has given <u>verifiable</u> proof of supernatural revelation. This is in the form of <u>already-fulfilled prophecies:</u> the prediction of events which happened after the prophecy was made, and which then occurred as they were predicted. We have historical proof that the prophecy was made before the event occurred, and historical proof that the event did indeed occur as was predicted. These were amazing predictions which could have only been made by God communicating supernatural truth to a prophet.

- Some of these astounding, already-fulfilled prophecies will be detailed in the next chapter, "Fulfilled Prophecies".

2. <u>We then know that the Bible is the written revelation</u> in which God has revealed His important and secret truths, because the already-fulfilled prophecies constitute verifiable proof of supernatural revelation. It is not a book of man's opinions, but of God's truths.

3. Consequently, <u>we can trust the Bible for the other, non-verifiable prophecies and eternal truths that are written within its pages.</u> The statements about the future and eternal-life can be trusted, because God has proven that the Bible is the place in which He has revealed His secrets. This is faith in what we cannot see, based on a verifiable source.

Therefore, as described above, <u>God's method is to provide **verifiable** evidence that the Bible reveals His truths, so that we can trust what it says about **unverifiable** concepts and instructions.</u>

Faith based on evidence

It is commendable that you have asked for evidence of eternal truths, and do not want to be forced into a "blind faith". You do not want to be gullible or tricked, but want to know who or what you can trust. Moreover, I hope that you are sincere in your desire for evidence, and will say, "Tell me mysteries from the past that nobody could have known, but that I can verify, and I will then trust what the Bible says about the future".

The existence of God has been demonstrated physically and logically in previous chapters. However, to be honest, I cannot prove to you directly that you can have eternal life, that Jesus' death on a cross actually paid for your sins, and that believing upon this is the means of obtaining forgiveness and eternal life.

You will have to personally decide whether to have faith in these teachings, but this can be a very confident faith. Having faith will be based on your own personal examination of the evidence for verifiable statements in the Bible, and then your own personal decision to believe the Bible for the unverifiable concepts about eternal life.

In chapter 8, Hebrews 11:1 was quoted as describing faith as the combination of being convinced of something unseen, and a decision to rely on that truth as something critical. I now want you to understand that this can be based on evidence, a <u>faith based on a written revelation that has been proven to be true.</u>

The task of a truth-seeker is to look at the "evidential" things to decide what can be trusted as revelation. Although you will never prove directly the biblical teachings about eternal life, you can come to a confident knowledge of them by faith.

Faith is trusting what the Bible says, taking its teachings and instructions as revealed truth directly from God. One can believe the Bible is true because of the verifiable evidence, using faith to take as true the unverifiable concepts. The Bible is trustworthy because it has accurately revealed mysteries regarding already-fulfilled prophecies.

Case Study: A King and a Prophet

We can illustrate the preceding verification principle by looking into a specific example that God has provided in the Bible. An historical story in the book of Daniel is relevant for our discussion about verifying a trustworthy source of supernatural revelation. I am not presenting this as proof of the Bible, but as a fascinating example which demonstrates what God has intentionally planned and provided for evidence and faith.

Nebuchadnezzar was an historical king of the Babylonian Empire, and we know much about him from archaeology, the Bible, and other writings. The story below is from the second chapter of the biblical book written by Daniel, who was a prophet of God.

> *Now in the second year of the reign of Nebuchadnezzar, Nebuchadnezzar had dreams; and his spirit was troubled and his sleep left him. Then the king gave orders to call in <u>the magicians, the conjurers, the sorcerers and the Chaldeans</u>, to tell the king his dreams. So they came in and stood before the king. And the king said to them, "I had a dream, and <u>my spirit is anxious to understand the dream</u>." (Daniel 2:1-3)*

The King Demands Evidence

King "Neb" (as I will call him) knew that there was something special about this dream, that it probably had a supernatural source and was intended to tell him something important. He wanted to know the significance, and he quickly became an honest seeker of supernatural revelation. Usually, people will not discover supernatural truths unless they are actually looking for them. He started his search by calling in all of the reputable intellectuals and wise men of his kingdom.

> *Then the Chaldeans spoke to the king in Aramaic: "O king, live forever! <u>Tell the dream </u>to your servants, and<u> we will declare</u> the interpretation." The king answered and said to the Chaldeans, "The command from me is firm: if you do not<u> make known to me the dream</u> and its<u> interpretation</u>, you will be torn limb from limb, and your houses will be made a rubbish heap." (Daniel 2:4-5)*

<u>Primarily, Neb wanted to know the interpretation</u> of the dream: the meaning that would tell him something important about the future. He already knew what the actual dream was. Nevertheless, he set an "evidence" condition, because he knew that people can claim to tell the truth but actually be lying. So he said that if they could not tell him the dream as well as the interpretation, then he would not believe them. He required that they prove to him that they were revealers of supernatural revelation.

He wanted to know what the dream prophesied, but the "test" was to tell him the dream. "Tell me the mystery that nobody could have known, but that I can verify, and I will then trust what you say about the future." He didn't just want to trust anyone who might tell him, but wanted proof that they had access to supernatural secrets. Most importantly, this is because King Neb really had an earnest desire to know the future.

> *The king replied, "I know for certain that you are bargaining for time, inasmuch as you have seen that the command from me is firm, that if you do not make the dream known to me, there is only one decree for you. For you have agreed together<u> to speak lying and corrupt words before me</u> until the situation is changed; therefore <u>tell me the dream, that I may know that you can declare to me its interpretation."</u> (Daniel 2:8-9)*

No False Prophecies or Interpretations

The so-called truth and wisdom of these men were lies, and Neb clearly saw this. He did not want to be tricked, and did not want a false or invented interpretation of his dream, not even a "happy" one, such as: "O King, this means you will be great and have eternal life". He was not interested in a religion that would be an illusory self-help trick for temporal happiness; he really wanted to know the truth! And this is exactly what God wants to provide for us today: not a man-made religion, but a God-given set of truths that we can trust.

Neb honestly wanted to know if the future would be good or bad, and what he could do about it. In order to achieve this, he knew that a good test would be the knowledge of something that no human could know on his own. He could see that these wise men were only lying and stalling for time.

In the biblical book of Isaiah, God makes clear His attitude toward false prophets and false religions:

> *Let them bring forth and <u>declare to us what is going to take place</u>; As for the <u>former [events], declare what they [were]</u>,That we may consider them and know their outcome. Or announce to us what is coming;*
> <u>*Declare the things that are going to come afterward,*</u>
> <u>*That we may know*</u> **that you are gods**...
> *(Isaiah 41:22-23)*

There have been many false prophets and religions. God is firm about an accurate understanding of truth, and warns people that they are making a big mistake to follow a group or a book that tells them lies and makes false promises. It is proper to demand valid reasons for trusting them with the truth.

Some Mysteries Can Only be Declared by God

The wise men then started talking to Neb about "the gods":

> *The Chaldeans answered the king and said, "<u>There is not a man on earth who could declare the matter</u> for the king, inasmuch as no great king or ruler has [ever] asked anything like this of any magician, conjurer or Chaldean. Moreover, the thing which the king demands is difficult, and there is no one else who could declare it to the king <u>except gods, whose dwelling place is not with [mortal] flesh</u>." (Daniel 2:10-11)*

The wise men were saying, "What you're asking is humanly impossible; no man can do it; we can't know what was in your mind while you were dreaming". Of course this confirms Neb's theory that this was a good test of something beyond human capabilities!

They stated clearly that no one "except gods" could declare these things, because perhaps they do know truths and mysteries. However, the wise men indicated their belief that the gods don't reveal mysteries to humans – perhaps they just can't be bothered, or they just don't care about people. Of course many people today think that perhaps God exists, but He doesn't reveal truth or communicate to people. There might be a "Creator", but there is not a "Revealer".

Having a lot of intelligence and experience wasn't good enough for these wise men, because they didn't have access to eternal truths. Their method of acquiring truth was finite and limited to what they could physically access, just like many scientists and philosophers today.

> *Because of this the king became indignant and very furious and gave orders to destroy all the wise men of Babylon. (Daniel 2:12)*

This was extremely frustrating and despairing for Neb. He was so furious that he wanted to destroy all the wise men. He had decided that if there is no supernatural revelation, then the wisdom of this world is not worth anything. It seemed that all knowledge was temporal, and the "interpretation" (meaning) was only an illusion.

God Willingly Reveals Mysteries through His Prophets

But then we have a transition in the story to a true prophet and revealed truth from God.

> *Then <u>the mystery was revealed to Daniel</u> in a night vision. Then Daniel blessed the God of heaven; Daniel said,*
> *"Let the name of God be blessed forever and ever,*
> *For wisdom and power belong to Him.*
> *It is He who changes the times and the epochs;*
> *He removes kings and establishes kings;*
> *He gives wisdom to wise men*
> *And knowledge to men of understanding.*
> *It is <u>He who reveals the profound and hidden things</u>;*
> *He knows what is in the darkness,*
> *And the light dwells with Him." (Daniel 2:19-22)*

God does reveal mysteries, and the secret was revealed to Daniel. Wisdom and knowledge are God's; He gives wisdom, and reveals deep and secret things. <u>He is willing to reveal to men.</u> Obviously, there is a large difference between Daniel and the wise men in their attitude toward God's willingness to reveal truth, and in seeking Him for that truth.

> *Daniel answered before the king and said, "As for the mystery about which the king has inquired, <u>neither wise men, conjurers, magicians [nor] diviners are able to declare [it] to the king.</u> However,<u> there is a God in heaven who reveals mysteries, and He has made known</u> to King Nebuchadnezzar what will take place in the latter days. This was your dream and the visions in your mind [while] on your bed. As for you, O king, [while] on your bed your thoughts turned to what would take place in the future; and He who reveals mysteries has made known to you what will take place. But as for me, this mystery has <u>not been revealed to me for any wisdom residing in me more than [in] any [other] living man, but for the purpose of making the interpretation known to the king</u>, and that you may understand the thoughts of your mind."*
> (Daniel 2:27-30)

What a beautiful and encouraging statement... *"there is a God in heaven who reveals mysteries, and He has made known..."* God exists, He does provide revelation, and He has communicated truth to men. He is a personal God who thinks and communicates and has plans for the future.

The King Believes in God and Trusts the Prophet

Neb had basically said, "Prove to me you can reveal mysteries from the past, and I will trust that you can tell me the future". Happily, here he was given evidence that God does indeed give direct revelation of secrets, and that he actually has "purposed" to do so. He wanted Neb to seek evidence, and He had intended all along to provide it. He wanted to prove that Daniel could tell the interpretation, by demonstrating that he was also able to tell the dream. God's purpose in telling Daniel the dream was so that Neb would believe the interpretation coming from Daniel, the prophet of God.

> "the great God has made known to the king what will take place in the future; so the dream is true and its interpretation is trustworthy." Then King Nebuchadnezzar fell on his face and did homage to Daniel, and gave orders to present to him an offering and fragrant incense. The king answered Daniel and said, <u>"Surely your God is a God of gods and a Lord of kings and a revealer of mysteries, since you have been able to reveal this mystery."</u>
> (Daniel 2:45 - 47)

This shows the enthusiastic response of an honest seeker when he has been shown proof. The dream was accurately revealed by God's prophet, so the interpretation presented by that prophet is trustworthy.

Some of the wise men also responded in faith

Let us look briefly at an additional note on this story from several centuries later. It is fascinating to see that 600 years after the story above, some wise men called the "magi" travelled to Jerusalem. These men were looking for the Messiah that had been prophesied by this same Daniel. They came at just the right time to see the young child Jesus, who had been born in a small village near Jerusalem.

The wise men mentioned above in the story of Nebuchadnezzar as the "magicians" were a group called the "magi". The wise men looking for Jesus 600 years later were probably a later generation of this same group of wise men from Babylon.

The book of Daniel mentions something very interesting about the relationship of Daniel with the magi (magicians):

> " And King Nebuchadnezzar, your father, your father the king, <u>appointed him chief of the magicians</u>, conjurers, Chaldeans [and] diviners." (Daniel 5:11)

Daniel had become leader of the magi after the interpretation of Nebuchadnezzar's dream. He also made specific prophecies about the coming of the Messiah, and the astounding significance of His life. He even predicted the timing of His appearance, so the magi probably came because of Daniel's specific prophecies.

It is encouraging to see that Daniel not only had an impact on King Nebuchadnezzar, but that he evidently had a large impact on the Babylonian wise men, as well--those men who did not think that God could or would communicate to men. Part of God's purpose was that the wise men would also see His evidence and decide to trust in Daniel's revealed truth. It seems that some of them, and perhaps a lot of them, did indeed change their minds.

I sincerely desire that many of today's "wise men" would also examine the evidence regarding God's revelation, and decide to believe both that God is willing to communicate to men and that He has already done so in the Bible.

In the next chapter, we will see that this "timing" of the Messiah is one of the amazing already-fulfilled prophecies of the Bible. This prophecy was actually made by Daniel himself, accurately specifying when the Messiah would come. Thus, seeing God's revealed purpose regarding the revelation of truth, we will now transition to an examination of this specific prophecy from Daniel, as well as other already-fulfilled prophecies.

Chapter 10
Fulfilled Prophecies

Many biblical predictions have already been accurately fulfilled. These prophecies are beyond human ability and provide evidence of intentional supernatural revelation.

God has intentionally provided evidence that the Bible is His written revelation of truth. An important part of this evidence is a set of written predictions (prophecies) which were fulfilled after the prediction was made. Since these have already been fulfilled, we can examine them and compare the prophecy with the fulfillment. I hope that you will be a "seeker" (as described in chapter 8) and consider these openly, looking for verifiable proof of supernatural revelation. Perhaps you will have the enthusiastic response of Nebuchadnezzar (chapter 9), as well as the wise men who eventually accepted the evidence and believed the eternal truths written by Daniel.

A) The Destruction of the City of Tyre

Many prophecies in the Bible are in reference to countries and cities. A bold and fascinating set of predictions was made by the prophet Ezekiel in the year 588 B.C., and was written in the biblical book of Ezekiel, chapter 26. Key parts of the prophecy are highlighted in the following passage:

Ezekiel 26:
- 3: *therefore thus says the Lord God, `Behold, I am against you, O Tyre, and I will bring up many nations against you, as the sea brings up its waves.*
- 4: *And they will <u>destroy the walls of Tyre and break down her towers</u>*
- 4: *I will <u>scrape her debris from her and make her a bare rock</u>.*
- 5: *She <u>will be a place for the spreading of nets in the midst of the sea</u>,*
- 7: *Behold, I will bring upon Tyre <u>from the north Nebuchadnezzar king of Babylon</u>, king of kings, with horses, chariots, cavalry, and a great army.*
- 12: *Also they will make a spoil of your riches and a prey of your merchandise, break down your walls and destroy your pleasant houses, and <u>throw your stones and your timbers and your debris into the water</u>.*
- 14: *I will <u>make you a bare rock; you will be a place for the spreading of nets</u>. You will be <u>built no more</u>, for I the Lord have spoken," declares the Lord God.*
- 19: *<u>I shall bring up the deep over you, and the great waters will cover you</u>,*

These statements are very specific, and have several amazing fulfillments which we will examine in detail. The city which was called Tyre in 588 B.C. was on the mainland, on the coast of the Mediterranean. This is not to be confused with the later (and current) city of the same name which is on a peninsula right next to the old city, although both cities play prominent parts in the fulfillment of the prophecy.

The city which is now called Tyre is on the lower left corner of the following map. It is located on the Mediterranean Sea, in the country of Lebanon, and just north of Israel.

Figure 13 [15]

The prophecy is made up of several specific predictions. These are described in separate sections below, along with their fulfillments.

1) **Destroyed:** Prediction that the city would be conquered and destroyed.

Ezekiel 26:
> 4: 'And they will <u>destroy the walls of Tyre and break down her towers</u>
> 7: "Behold, I will bring upon Tyre <u>from the north Nebuchadnezzar king of Babylon</u>, king of kings, with horses, chariots, cavalry, and a great army."

The fulfillment of this prediction was accomplished a few years later, when <u>Nebuchadnezzar</u> (whom we discussed in chapter 9) attacked. He laid siege for 13 years and finally conquered and <u>destroyed the city</u>.

Historical evidence for this is presented in the book, "Babylonian Life And History" (E. A. Wallis Budge):
- ➢ "Nebuchadnezzar took all Palestine and Syria and the cities on the seacoast, including Tyre, which fell after a siege of 13 years (573 B.C.)" [16]

2) **Into the Water:** Predictions that the ruins of the city would be thrown into the water.

Ezekiel 26:
- ➢ *12: Also they will make a spoil of your riches and a prey of your merchandise, break down your walls and destroy your pleasant houses, and <u>throw your stones and your timbers and your debris into the water.</u>*
- ➢ *4: I will <u>scrape her debris from her and make her a bare rock</u>.*
- ➢ *19: <u>I shall bring up the deep over you, and the great waters will cover you,</u>*

These predictions are more specific and striking, stating that the materials from the former city would be thrown into the water, and the site of the city would become a bare rock. The fulfillment came more than 200 years later, when Alexander the Great attacked an island off the coast.

Most of the survivors from the destroyed city of Tyre (and then their descendants) had moved to an island about a half-mile from the coast, and had named the island city "Tyre". In 333 B.C., Alexander the Great demanded the surrender of the island city, but they refused as they were confident he could not mount a sufficient seaborne attack.

Alexander did not have adequate ships, so he decided upon a novel strategy. As shown in the diagram below, this involved building a land causeway (called a "mole") out to the island, so that he could march his army up to the city. He needed a large quantity of physical material to throw into the sea in order to form a mass that was one-half mile long and 200 feet wide. Since this was near the site and remains of old Tyre, he used the <u>debris and materials from the old city of Tyre to build the causeway, throwing them into the water</u>. The <u>old city was scraped clean, and only a bare rock remained.</u>

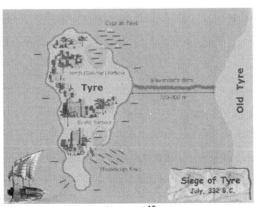

Figure 14 [17]

A source of historical evidence for these events is the first-century historian *Quintus Curtius Rufus* :
- *Envoys from Tyre offended Alexander, and he decided to lay siege (Rufus, 4.2.3-5)*
- *The Tyrians were confident that their island could withstand a siege (Rufus, 4.2.6-7, 12, 15)*
- *Alexander's soldiers built a mole from the mainland to the island (Rufus, 4.2.19-21)*
- *A large amount of rock was used from the old city of Tyre on the mainland (Rufus, 4.2.18).* [18]

In his book *Alexander of Macedon*, Peter Green states that:
> "Today, deep under asphalt streets and apartment blocks, the stone core of that fantastic causeway still stands: one of Alexander's most tangible and permanent legacies to posterity." [19]

This was a fantastic event, and an amazing fulfillment of the prophetic details. The method of fulfillment could not have been predicted by men, but was illustrative of the secret knowledge and plans of God. The picture below, from 1934, shows the island city and the man-made causeway (the causeway is now much wider).

Figure 15 [20]

3) **Midst of the Sea**

Ezekiel 26
> 5: 'She <u>will be a place for the spreading of nets</u> <u>in the midst of the sea</u>,

One detail of this prediction in verse 5 is that Tyre would be "in the midst of the sea". This would have been very confusing to a

reader of the prophecy until its fulfillment by Alexander's army throwing the city ruins into the Mediterranean. The tour book called *"Your Guide to Lebanon"* states:
> ➤ *"The <u>ruins</u> of ancient Tyre are different from all the others – <u>situated… in the heart of the sea</u>"*. [21]

This represents both an amazing prediction and a fantastic fulfillment, accomplished through Alexander's unusual attack of the island city.

As for the other part of verse 5's prediction, fishermen do spread their nets on the causeway, which is of course on the ruins of Tyre. Notice that this is separate from the prediction in verse 14 below, that fishermen would spread their nets on the bare rock that was the site of the old city.

4) **The Site:** A bare rock for the spreading of nets

Ezekiel 26
> ➤ 14: I will <u>make you a bare rock; you will be a place for the spreading of nets</u>

In his textbook, *"General History for Colleges and High Schools"*, Phillip Myers states that:
> ➤ "Alexander the Great reduced Tyre to ruins in 332 BC. Tyre recovered in a measure from this blow, but never regained the place she had previously held in the world. The larger part of the <u>site of the once great city is now as bare as the top of a rock -- a place where the fishermen that still frequent the spot spread their nets to dry</u>". [22]

The latter part of this statement by Phillip Myers reads almost exactly like the prediction in verse 14, that the site would become a bare rock, and a place for the spreading of nets. The causeway has now grown much wider because of the accumulation of sand and silt, and the island city has expanded throughout the causeway, becoming a continuous city reaching to the shore. Thus, it all appears now as one continuous section of land. The city is on the island and causeway, but the portion on the mainland (site of the old city) is still as bare as a rock.

5) Never Rebuilt

Ezekiel 26
> ➢ *14: You will be <u>built no more</u>,*

Although it has now been more than 2,500 years since Tyre was destroyed, it has never been rebuilt. As described above, there are not even any ruins left at the site, but it is as bare as a rock. The island city took the name of Tyre, but a city has not been rebuilt at the location where the old city was destroyed.

Conclusions from the Prophecy of Tyre

I have included above many details of the predictions, fulfillments, and historical evidence for the prophecy about Tyre, in order to provide a thorough example of God's intentional evidence for the Bible as His written communication of supernatural revelation. The predictions demonstrate foreknowledge which was beyond human ability, and the fulfillments themselves also demonstrate supernatural direction of events. Moreover, the historical sources help to provide verifiable evidence, fitting into God's purpose to provide a method and means for faith in the Bible's statements about the future and eternal life.

B) Timing of the Messiah in Jerusalem

A large number of prophecies in the Bible predict details about the coming of the "Messiah" (or "Christ"), who would save people from their sins. Christians believe that these already-fulfilled prophecies not only provide evidence that the Bible is the revelation of God – they also demonstrate that Jesus is the Messiah, because they were accurately fulfilled by Him.

I will present and describe a prophecy which is written in the book of Daniel, and which Daniel says was told to him by an angel of God. This is an amazing prediction as to the timing of the coming of the Messiah.

> *So you are to know and discern that from the issuing of a decree to restore and rebuild Jerusalem until Messiah the Prince there will be seven weeks and sixty- two weeks; it will be built again, with plaza and moat, even in times of distress. Then after the sixty- two weeks the Messiah will be cut off and have nothing… (Daniel 9:25-26)*

Evidence for when the prophecy was written

Some of the prophecies in the book of Daniel are so specific and accurate that critics have claimed the book was written after the events that fulfilled these predictions. However, there are sources that prove copies of the book were circulating hundreds of years before the time of Jesus Christ:

- Josephus, the excellent first-century historian for the Romans, tells us that in 333 B.C, Alexander the Great was shown a copy of Daniel by Jewish leaders after he entered Jerusalem ("Antiquities of the Jews", Book XI)[23]
- The Septuagint, a translation of the Jewish Scriptures from Hebrew into Greek, was compiled in approximately 250 B.C. and contains the book of Daniel
- The Dead Sea Scrolls contain copies of portions of Daniel from before the time of Jesus.

Details of the prophecy

We are told in verse 25 that Messiah "the Prince" would come 69 weeks after the decree to rebuild Jerusalem (which had been destroyed by the Babylonians). The word "weeks" literally means "sevens", and can either mean "seven days" or "seven years". This prophecy is in terms of years. Therefore, the time given is 69 seven-year periods, which is 483 years. The following passage from the biblical book of Revelation makes it clear that these are 360-day years:

> "And I will grant [authority] to my two witnesses, and they will prophesy for <u>twelve hundred and sixty days</u>, clothed in sackcloth." (Revelation 11:3)

This passage describes one-half of the final seven years. Since the three-and-one-half year period has 1260 days, then each year has exactly 360 days.

The decree to rebuild Jerusalem is recorded in the Biblical book of Nehemiah, chapter 2, verses 1-8. It was made by Artaxerxes Longimanus, king of the Persians. We know from historical records discovered in the king's palace in Susa (the capital of Persia), by Sir Henry Creswicke Rawlinson, that the decree was made in 445 B.C. Nehemiah tells us this was the month of Nisan (March/April).[24]

So this bold and specific prophecy tells us that the Messiah would enter Jerusalem as "the Prince" 483 360-day years after the month of Nisan in 445 B.C.

The Fulfillment of the Prophecy

The prediction takes us to the year 32 A.D., in the month of April, using our 365-day calendar. The coming of the Messiah as "the

Prince" was fulfilled when Jesus entered Jerusalem on Palm Sunday, with a large crowd welcoming Him as the King of Israel:

> *On the next day the large crowd who had come to the feast, when they heard that Jesus was coming to Jerusalem, took the branches of the palm trees and went out to meet Him, and [began] to shout, "Hosanna! Blessed is He who comes in the name of the Lord, even the King of Israel." (John 12:12-13)*

The second event mentioned in Daniel's prophecy regarded the Messiah being "cut off".

> *Then after the sixty-two weeks the Messiah will be cut off and have nothing. (Daniel 9:26)*

This predicted the specific timing of the death of the Messiah, and was fulfilled just a few days after Palm Sunday, when Jesus was executed on a cross by the Romans.

The Historical Timing

We know the timing of these events in the life and death of Jesus from other historical sources regarding people and events mentioned in the Bible, such as the acting Roman governor (Pontius Pilate) and the Jewish high priest. The biblical book of Luke places the timing of the beginning of Jesus' public ministry by clear references to several historical figures:

> *Now in the fifteenth year of the reign of Tiberius Caesar, when Pontius Pilate was governor of Judea, and Herod was tetrarch of Galilee, and his brother Philip was tetrarch of the region of Ituraea and Trachonitis, and Lysanias was tetrarch of Abilene, in the high priesthood of Annas and Caiaphas, the word of God came to John, the son of Zacharias, in the wilderness. (Luke 3:1-2)*

Obviously, this passage is intentionally providing verifiable evidence in regard to the specific historic setting. The detail regarding the "fifteenth year of the reign of Tiberius Caesar" is especially helpful for dating:

- *"Now the date of Tiberius Caesar's reign is known with absolute accuracy; and his fifteenth year, reckoned from his accession, began on the 19th August, A.D. 28."* (Sir Robert Anderson, The Coming Prince)[25]
- Jesus' crucifixion was a little over three years after the beginning of His public ministry, at Passover time. This places the year of Jesus' entry into Jerusalem as the Messiah at 32 A.D.[26]

Conclusions from the Prophecy of the Timing of the Messiah

This prophecy regarding the year and month of the coming of the Messiah is striking in specificity and accuracy, and demonstrates both a supernatural prediction and a supernatural fulfillment. Historical evidence shows clearly that the prophecy was made several hundred years in advance of its fulfillment.

The written record in the book of Daniel was purposely designed by God to provide proof that the Bible is the place where He communicates supernatural truth. The revelation provided to Daniel for Nebuchadnezzar (described in chapter 9) convinced the king and the wise men that they could trust Daniel's prophecies about the near future, and the predictions of the coming Messiah provide us today with verifiable evidence that we can trust the Bible concerning the eternal future.

C) Other Messianic Prophecies

There are over 200 prophecies in the Bible concerning the Messiah, many of which have already been fulfilled. Because of the amazing accuracy of these predictions, many Bible critics had claimed that the prophecies were actually written after their fulfillments in the first-century A.D.

However, the discovery of the Dead Sea Scrolls in 1947 contained copies of several books of the Bible with many of the prophecies below, and many of those scrolls were dated to before the time that Jesus lived. This is clear evidence that the predictions were written before their fulfillment in the life, death, and resurrection of Jesus Christ.

The following table presents several Messianic prophecies which were fulfilled in Jesus. In addition to providing evidence that the Bible is the revelation of God, these prophecies prove that Jesus is the Messiah, and that the Jewish "Old Testament" and Christian "New Testament" are the two parts of a unified revelation from God.

Messianic Prophecies of the Bible

Prophecy	Old Testament	New Testament
Child would be Born who is the Mighty God	Isaiah 9:6 For a <u>child</u> will be <u>born</u> to us, a <u>son</u> will be given to us; And the government will rest on His shoulders; And His name will be called Wonderful Counselor, <u>Mighty God</u>, <u>Eternal Father</u>, Prince of Peace."	John 1:14 And the Word <u>became flesh</u>, and dwelt among us, and we beheld His glory, glory as of the <u>only begotten from the Father</u>, full of grace and truth. Luke 2:11 for today in the city of David there has been <u>born for you a Savior</u>, who is <u>Christ the Lord</u>.
Place of Birth	Micah 5:2 "But as for you, <u>Bethlehem Ephrathah</u>, [Too] <u>little</u> to be among the clans of Judah, From you One will go forth for Me to be <u>ruler in Israel</u>. His goings forth are from long ago, <u>From the days of eternity</u>."	Matthew 2:1 Now after Jesus was born in <u>Bethlehem of Judea</u>…
Christ would die, then Jerusalem and the temple would be destroyed	Daniel 9:26 "Then after the sixty-two weeks the <u>Messiah will be cut off</u> and have nothing, and the people of the prince who is to come will <u>destroy the city and the sanctuary</u>. And its end [will come] with a flood; even to the end there will be war; desolations are determined	Jesus Christ died in AD 33. The Romans destroyed Jerusalem and the temple in AD 70.
Method of Death: Crucifixion: The hands and feet were pierced by nails; hung from a cross	Psalm 22:16 For dogs have surrounded me; A band of evildoers has encompassed me; They <u>pierced</u> my <u>hands</u> and my <u>feet</u>.	Luke 23:33 And when they came to the place called The Skull, there <u>they crucified him</u> and the criminals…

Prophecy	Old Testament	New Testament
Water would pour out of Him; His heart would burst (caused the blood and water)	Psalm 22:14 I am <u>poured out like water</u>, And all my bones are out of joint; <u>My heart is like wax</u>; it is <u>melted within me</u>.	John 19:34 but one of the soldiers pierced His side with a spear, and immediately <u>there came out blood and water</u>.
A close friend would betray Him	Psalm 41:7 All who hate me <u>whisper together against me</u>; Against me they <u>devise my hurt</u>, [saying,] 8 "A wicked thing is poured out upon him, <u>That when he lies down, he will not rise up again</u>." 9 <u>Even my close friend, in whom I trusted, Who ate my bread</u>, Has lifted up his heel against me.	Matthew 26:14 Then <u>one of the twelve</u>, named Judas Iscariot, went to the <u>chief priests</u>, 15 and said, "What are you willing to give me <u>to deliver Him up to you</u>?" And they weighed out to him thirty pieces of silver.
Betrayed for 30 Pieces of Silver; Threw money into the Temple; Money went to a Potter	Zechariah 11:12 And I said to them, "If it is good in your sight, give [me] my wages; but if not, never mind!" So they weighed out <u>thirty</u> [shekels] <u>of silver</u> as my wages. 13 Then the Lord said to me, "<u>Throw it to the potter</u>, [that] magnificent <u>price at which I was valued</u> by them." So I took the <u>thirty</u> [shekels] <u>of silver</u> and <u>threw them</u> to the <u>potter</u> in the <u>house of the Lord</u>.	Matthew 26:15 ...And they weighed out to him <u>thirty pieces of silver</u>. Matt 27:5 And he <u>threw</u> the pieces of silver <u>into the sanctuary</u>... Matt 27:7 And they counseled together and with the money <u>bought the potter's field</u> as a burial place for strangers.

Prophecy	Old Testament	New Testament
Some of His Clothes Divided; For Others Lots were Cast	Psalm 22:18 They <u>divide my garments</u> among them, And for my <u>clothing they cast lots.</u>	John 19:23 The soldiers therefore, when they had crucified Jesus, took His <u>outer garments and made four parts</u>, a part to every soldier and [also] the tunic; <u>now the tunic was seamless, woven in one piece.</u> 24 They said therefore to one another, "Let us not tear it, but <u>cast lots</u> for it, [to decide] whose it shall be"…
He would go to Egypt while young	Hosea 11:1 When Israel [was] a <u>youth</u> I loved him, And <u>out of Egypt I called My son.</u>	Matthew 2:14 And he arose and took the <u>Child and His mother</u> by night, and departed for <u>Egypt</u>; 15 and was there <u>until the death of Herod</u>…
Incredible Thirst while He was Dying	Psalm 22:15 My strength is dried up like a potsherd, And <u>my tongue cleaves to my jaws</u>; And Thou dost lay me in the dust of <u>death</u>.	John 19:28 After this, Jesus, knowing that all things had already been accomplished, in order that the Scripture might be fulfilled, said, "<u>I am thirsty</u>."
He would be scourged	Isaiah 53:5 …And by His <u>scourging</u> we are healed.	Matthew 27:26 Then he released Barabbas for them; but after having Jesus <u>scourged</u>, he delivered Him to be crucified.
They would Spit on Him and Beat Him	Isaiah 50:6 I gave My back to those who <u>strike</u> [Me,] And My cheeks to those who pluck out the beard; I did not cover My face from humiliation and <u>spitting</u>.	Matthew 26:67 Then they <u>spat</u> in His face and <u>beat</u> Him with their fists; and others slapped Him,…

Prophecy	Old Testament	New Testament
With a rich man in His death	Isaiah 53:9 His grave was assigned with wicked men, Yet He was <u>with a rich man in His death</u>,	Matthew 27:57 When it was evening, there came a <u>rich man</u> from Arimathea, named Joseph, who himself had also become a disciple of Jesus. 58 This man went to Pilate and asked for the body of Jesus. Then Pilate ordered it to be given to him. 59 And Joseph took <u>the body</u> and wrapped it in a clean linen cloth, 60 and laid it in his <u>own new tomb</u>

Some of the predictions in this table are from two chapters of the Bible which were written more than 700 years before the life of Jesus, but have striking descriptions of both His death and His intentional purpose. Psalm 22 has a vivid description of the manner in which Jesus would be executed (even though crucifixions had not yet been performed). Isaiah 53 describes the reason and accomplishment of His death. I encourage you to read through both of these chapters for supernatural prophetic insight into this very crucial event.

Conclusions from the Prophecies of the Messiah

The correlation above between the Old and New Testaments of the Bible is clear demonstration of the principle articulated in chapter 9: verifiable evidence through fulfilled prophecy, providing for knowledge-based faith in eternal truth. The Old Testament has many prophecies which were already fulfilled in the New Testament, and most of these predictions are focused on the Messiah. The verifiable fulfillments prove that Jesus is the Messiah, and they enable us to trust in the significant promises for eternal life, which are also focused on Jesus Christ.

Verified Revelation we can Trust

In this chapter we have seen several amazing predictions which could have only been made by God communicating supernatural truth to a prophet. Through these, <u>we know that the Bible is the written revelation in which God reveals His important and secret truths</u>, because the already-fulfilled prophecies constitute verifiable proof of supernatural revelation. Consequently, <u>we can trust the Bible for the other, non-verifiable prophecies and eternal truths that are written within its pages.</u>

It can also be observed that the availability of the Bible is what would be expected of a written communication directed and preserved by God. It is the best-selling book of all time, was the first to be printed on the Gutenberg press in the 15th century, and continues to be the most popular book each year. It has also been translated into more languages than any other book in history. Currently part or all of the Bible is available in over 2,000 languages.

Our goal as stated in Chapter 7 is to learn about eternity-future. We have now established that the tool to do that is the Bible. Its statements about the future and eternal life can be trusted, because God has proven that the Bible is the place in which He reveals His secrets.

Part 4: Eternity-Future

Chapter 11
The Book from God

Looking into God's revelation

"The unfolding of Your words gives light"
Psa 119:130

We have reached another significant milestone in our discovery process, and are finally at the point where we can learn directly about eternity-future. Thus far we have depended on a combination of physical evidence and deductive reasoning for a foundation from the past, but now we can look into the Bible for direct communication about the future.

Fortunately, God has indeed communicated to us, in written form. Even before looking into the content of the Bible, the fact that He has chosen to reveal truth to us is very encouraging in several ways. This means that He <u>wants</u> to "talk" to us, and also implies that He cares about us and has decided to offer us some sort of relationship with Himself. We can "hear" (in written form) the eternal God talking directly to us in an intelligent, clear, and intentional manner, and He has purposely revealed to us His plans for the future.

The communication is understandable to us, so that there is a coherent transfer of information, meaning, and even emotion from God's mind to ours. The communication is intelligent and reasoned, which is exactly what we should expect, since He created man and therefore has an intelligence superior to our own.

It is exciting to look into the Bible, and the inquiring mind can do so with eagerness. It makes sense that God is the one with the answers to all of the questions, as well as wonderful explanations of truths that we haven't even asked about. He has communicated extensively (the Bible is comprised of 66 books), and we find out about His desires, His rules, and His plans. We uncover the background and purposes of many events and principles.

Although we do not see Him, we discover that He is closely involved in human activities, and that He is *"not far from each one of us" (Acts 17:27)*. It is pleasing to know that He does indeed care about us: *"I have loved you with an everlasting love" (Jeremiah 31:3)*. Moreover, we are told that He has good intentions for our future: *"plans to prosper you and not to harm you, plans to give you hope and a future" (Jeremiah 29:11 (NIV))*. We learn that He is understanding of our weaknesses, temptations, and failures.

Looking to the Bible in faith does not mean the casting aside of intelligence. On the contrary, it is the only way to embark on a knowledge-based exploration of eternity-future, and is an intellectually-stimulating endeavor that involves all aspects of your mind.

Chapter 12
The Eternal Person

We learn about a person who has existed from eternity-past, lived as a man, and will live into eternity-future.

> *"And He is the image of the invisible God, the firstborn of all creation. For by Him all things were created, [both] in the heavens and on earth, visible and invisible…"*
> *Colossians 1:15-16*

The Son of God

As demonstrated in our look at already-fulfilled prophecies, the first part of the Bible (the "Old Testament") predicts the coming of the Messiah. The "New Testament" reveals Jesus as the Messiah, also called the "Christ". He is declared to be the Son of God, and the promises of God for eternity-future are centered on Him. We will look directly at a few passages of the Bible which describe Jesus Christ.

Personal Attributes

Several striking statements are made below about the nature, accomplishments, and significant purposes of Jesus Christ.

> *God, after He spoke long ago to the fathers in the prophets in many portions and in many ways, in these last days has spoken to us in His Son, whom He appointed heir of all things, through whom also He made the world.*
>
> *And He is the radiance of His glory and the exact representation of His nature, and upholds all things by the word of His power. When He had made purification of sins, He sat down at the right hand of the Majesty on high (Hebrews 1:1-3)*

He is the Son of God, having His exact nature. Through Jesus, God made the physical universe. He made "purification of sins", and currently He is seated in heaven at the right hand of God the Father. In addition, through Him God has communicated to us.

Life on Earth

The following Bible passage explains the context and purpose of Jesus' life on earth:

> *...Christ Jesus, who, although He existed in the form of God, did not regard equality with God a thing to be grasped, but emptied Himself, taking the form of a bond-servant, [and] being made in the likeness of men.*
>
> *Being found in appearance as a man, He humbled Himself by becoming obedient to the point of death, even death on a cross.*
>
> *For this reason also, God highly exalted Him, and bestowed on Him the name which is above every name, so that at the name of Jesus every knee will bow, of those who are in heaven and on earth and under the earth, and that every*

> *tongue will confess that Jesus Christ is Lord, to the glory of God the Father. (Phillippians 2:5-11)*

This passage tells us that He had always "existed in the form of God", and then took the form of a man. He voluntarily submitted Himself to death by crucifixion, the Roman form of execution by nailing a person to a wooden cross. However, He is now "highly exalted", and everyone will eventually submit to Him and acknowledge that He is "the Lord".

Eternal Life is in Him

The main purpose of our quest has been eternal life. In the passage below we are told clearly that <u>eternal life is in Jesus Christ</u>.

> *And the testimony is this, that God has given us eternal life, and <u>this life is in His Son.</u> <u>He who has the Son has the life;</u> he who does not have the Son of God does not have the life. These things I have written to you who believe in the name of the Son of God, so that you <u>may know that you have eternal life.</u> (1 John 5:11-13)*

We know that our physical bodies are decaying, and that something supernatural is needed to rescue us from that. We already deduced in chapter 4 that God is eternal and without decay, and also that He has complete control over the physical (He created the physical from nothing).

The Bible tells us that "he who has the Son has the life", so it is only by receiving something through the eternal Jesus that we will be able to live forever. Moreover, we see that God <u>wants</u> this to happen for us – He has been planning this for us, and He wants those who believe in Jesus to <u>know</u> that they have eternal life.

| Existence of God | Infinite Value | Revelation of Truth | **Eternity Future** |

Chapter 13
Eternity-Future

Eternal life is offered to every person,
and it is both spiritual and physical.

"I have loved you with an everlasting love"
Jeremiah 31:3

If atheism were true, then the future would be very bleak and depressing. Within a few decades, most of us alive today would cease to exist. The physical universe would continue its course to disorder (in accordance with the law of entropy) and become completely non-functional in a finite number of years.

However, it is exciting to know that God does exist, and we will look directly into His written revelation to uncover mysteries of the future. The Bible is God's written revelation and the clear communication of His intentions and instructions for men.

The primary purpose of the Bible is stated by the prophet John, near the end of his account of the life of Jesus:

> ...these have been written so that you may believe that Jesus is the Christ, the Son of God; and that believing you may have life in His name. (John 20:31)

A) Truth about Eternity-Future

Making all things new

At this time we are surrounded by temporary objects, and the permanent things are "not seen". This is why we currently know eternal items by faith and not by sight. However, according to the Bible the situation will change. We will see what is now invisible, and a new permanent world will be created for us.

> ...while we look not at the things which are seen, but at the things which are not seen; for the things which are seen are temporal, but the things which are not seen are eternal. (2 Corinthians 4:18)

> ...for we walk by faith, not by sight (2 Corinthians 5:7)

As described in the following passage, today's temporary and corruptible entities (such as our planet) will be replaced with those that are permanent.

> Then I saw a new heaven and a new earth; for the first heaven and the first earth passed away, and there is no longer any sea. And I saw the holy city, new Jerusalem, coming down out of heaven from God, made ready as a bride adorned for her husband. And I heard a loud voice from the throne, saying, "Behold, the tabernacle of God is among men, and He will dwell among them, and they shall be His people, and God Himself will be among them, and He will wipe away every tear from their eyes; and there will no longer be any death; there will no longer be any mourning, or crying, or pain; the first things have passed away." And He who sits on the throne said, "Behold, I am making all things new." (Revelation 21:1-5)

The universe will be turned into one that is eternal and without decay. God will no longer be invisible to men, but will have a close and active relationship with us. The sufferings of this life will be no more. We have been experiencing the "first things", but they will pass away, and everything will be new.

Eternity-future with God will be the ultimate value that we discussed in chapter 6 – a life in which each day is filled with love, beauty, and pleasure. This satisfies all of our deepest desires and will never end, but will continue on forever.

> *In Your presence is fullness of joy; In Your right hand there are pleasures forever. (Psalm 16:11)*

The Nature of Eternal Life

You might wonder how you could live forever, since your body will start to decay immediately after death. God provides an explanation of the nature of your own potential immortality. The Bible says that if you have met the necessary condition, then you are promised an eternal life which is both spiritual and physical.

The following passage emphasizes the spiritual aspect of eternal life. You have already been born physically (of water and the flesh). When you are granted eternal life, you are also given a spiritual birth, which enables you to live forever spiritually.

> *Jesus answered and said to him, "Truly, truly, I say to you, unless one is born again he cannot see the kingdom of God." Nicodemus ^said to Him, "How can a man be born when he is old? He cannot enter a second time into his mother's womb and be born, can he?" Jesus answered, "Truly, truly, I say to you, unless one is born of water and the Spirit he cannot enter into the kingdom of God. "That*

> *which is born of the flesh is flesh, and that which is born of the Spirit is spirit.* "Do not be amazed that I said to you, `You must be born again.' (John 3:3-7)*

For those who have been granted eternal life, there will also be a physical resurrection from the dead. This will take place in the future, bringing your physical body back to life, and uniting your spirit with your resurrected body.

> *... in order that I may attain to the resurrection from the dead. (Phillippians 3:10-11)*

When this physical resurrection happens, your corruptible body will be transformed into a body that will be incorruptible, and that will never die.

> *...the dead will be raised imperishable, and we will be changed. For this perishable must put on the imperishable, and this mortal must put on immortality.*
> *(1 Corinthians 15:52-53)*

Obviously your body might have undergone a very significant amount of decay before this happens. God does not tell us the details, but we know that He has complete control over the physical.

B) How to Obtain Eternal Life

The instructions in the Bible about obtaining eternal life are very simple and clear. In this section we will look at several verses to understand what God has already accomplished as well as His condition for us. God has promised eternal life to everyone who has faith in Jesus Christ for the forgiveness of sins.

Sin and Judgment

Sin is anything that falls short of God's perfect standard of obedience and behavior. All of us have done wrong and are below God's requirement of righteousness:

> *for all have sinned and fall short of the glory of God (Romans 3:23)*
>
> *For whoever keeps the whole law and yet stumbles in one point, he has become guilty of all.*
> *(James 2:10)*
>
> *Therefore, just as through one man sin entered into the world, and death through sin, and so death spread to all men, because all sinned—*
> *(Romans 5:12)*

Many people do not like to hear about sins and judgment, but that is similar to not wanting to go to the doctor because you might hear that you have cancer. You need to understand the problem in order to receive the solution:

> *And Jesus answered and said to them, "[It is] not those who are well who need a physician, but those who are sick. "I have not come to call the righteous but sinners to repentance." (Luke 5:31-32)*

Jesus said this to those who think that they have not committed any wrongs, but we are told clearly that "all have sinned". You can only receive righteousness from Jesus if you admit that you do not have it on your own.

Our sins will cause us to be separated from God for all of eternity, although it is clear that God does not want this to happen. In this passage, not "obeying" the gospel means not admitting your sins and trusting in Jesus Christ.

> *...dealing out retribution to those who do not know God and to those who do not obey the gospel of our Lord Jesus . These will pay the penalty of eternal destruction, away from the presence of the Lord and from the glory of His power (2 Thessalonians 1:8-9)*

The death and resurrection of Jesus Christ

The gospel ("good news") is that Jesus, the Son of God, voluntarily underwent a physical death for our sins. This happened when He was executed on a cross by the Romans. He was then physically resurrected three days later.

> *For I delivered to you as of first importance what I also received, that <u>Christ died for our sins</u> according to the Scriptures, and that <u>He was buried,</u> and that <u>He was raised on the third day</u> according to the Scriptures*
> *(1 Corinthians 15:3-4)*

Even though Jesus had never sinned, He died to receive the judgment for our sins. God's justice demands punishment for sins, and Jesus took our place to receive this punishment, resulting in righteousness for anyone who trusts in Him.

> *He made Him who knew no sin <u>to be sin on our behalf</u>, so that we might <u>become the righteousness of God in Him</u>.*
> *(2 Corinthians 5:21)*

God's love and compassion for us is so strong that the Son of God willingly offered Himself to take the form of a man and suffer death, in order that we could receive forgiveness of sins and have eternal life.

The only way to receive eternal life is through Jesus Christ. There is no religion, system, or good intentions which can accomplish this. God has laid out a single condition which is available to every person, and there is no other way.

> *And there is salvation in no one else ; for there is no other name under heaven that has been given among men by which we must be saved . (Acts 4:12)*

The condition for receiving eternal life

God's plan was to have Jesus die for you, and His condition for granting eternal life is that you believe that He died to pay for your own sins. As mentioned before, faith is the combination of being convinced of something unseen, and a decision to rely on that truth as something critical. By faith you know that Jesus died for you, and you rely on His death as the payment for your sins. (Note: "Believe" is just the verb-form of "faith", so they can be used interchangeably.)

> *For God so loved the world, that He gave His only begotten Son, that whoever believes in Him shall not perish, but have eternal life . (John 3:16)*

This is intentionally a simple condition that does not involve doing anything to "earn" eternal life, but just deciding to believe in order to "receive" it. In the verse below, the word "justify" means to make righteous. We are told that God forgives all of your sins and "credits" righteousness to you, when you believe personally in what Jesus did for you.

> *But to the one who does not work, but believes in Him who justifies the ungodly, his faith is credited as righteousness (Romans 4:5)*

God eagerly extends this offer to everyone, no matter what their background or religious upbringing has been. Receiving eternal life in Jesus Christ does not require a long process or any other conditions. You can receive it by faith immediately.

God emphatically makes the point that this is a free gift, and we do not perform any good deeds to earn eternal life. He wants us to clearly understand that Jesus did all the work, and our only role is to trust in what He did for us.

> *For by grace you have been saved through faith ; and that not of yourselves, it is the gift of God; not as a result of works, so that no one may boast. (Ephesians 2:8-9)*

If you have decided to put your faith in Jesus, it would be good to talk to God, and tell Him that you are trusting in Jesus' death on the cross for your own forgiveness of sins and eternal life. He will hear your prayer, as he knows everything that you say or even think.

> *..."Whoever will call on the name of the Lord will be saved." (Romans 10:13)*

Conclusion

In the Bible, God promises that if you believe who Jesus is and trust in Him for the forgiveness of your sins, then you are immediately credited with righteousness and are granted eternal life. You will not be judged for your sins, and in a sense you have already passed out of death and into life. He wants you to have eternal life, and He wants you to be confident that you do have it. Following is a solid promise from Jesus:

> *Truly, truly, I say to you, he who hears My word, and believes Him who sent Me, has eternal life, and does not come into judgment, but has passed out of death into life. (John 5:24)*

Eternal life is available to every person, and the condition for obtaining it is faith in Jesus Christ for the forgiveness of sins. For you personally, the offer is an infinite number of years in the presence of the Lord - with fullness of joy, fantastic pleasures, and the intense love of a self-giving God.

| Existence of God | Infinite Value | Revelation of Truth | Eternity Future |

Conclusion
Entering Eternal Life

*We arrive at an understanding of
the true history and destiny of our universe,
and look forward confidently to the
fantastic happiness of our eternal life.*

This Temporary Age

We are living in a temporary physical universe, and this time period can only be properly understood in the context of eternity and through the revelation of the Bible. Our planet experiences corruption and decay, and will eventually be incapable of supporting life. At the individual level, the body will eventually experience severe trauma or disease, ending our physical life. Despite difficulties and sufferings, most people want to go on living, and have an intense fear of death.

> *My heart is in anguish within me, And the terrors of death have fallen upon me. Fear and trembling come upon me… (Psalm 55:4-5)*

A common response is to attempt to ignore the coming death, and focus on pleasure. However, the Bible tells us that it is actually more beneficial to consider death than to ignore it. We should consider the fact that death is coming, and take it to heart.

> *It is <u>better to go to a house of mourning</u>*
> *Than to go to a house of feasting,*
> *<u>Because that is the end of every man,</u>*
> *<u>And the living takes it to heart.</u>*
> *Sorrow is better than laughter,*
> *For when a face is sad a heart may be happy.*
> *The mind of the wise is in the house of mourning,*
> *While the mind of fools is in the house of pleasure.*
> (Ecclesiastes 7:2-4)

Since God is unseen, many people have focused only on the visible temporal objects, choosing (whether explicitly or implicitly) to not look for the things which are invisible yet permanent. For many people, the truth of the eternal God has been replaced with the view that the universe and all life appeared on its own.

> *For they exchanged the truth of God for a lie, and worshiped and served the <u>creature</u> rather than the <u>Creator</u>, who is blessed forever. Amen. (Romans 1:25)*

God is patient, and does not immediately reject people for unbelief, but reaches out to them with evidence and reason. We can determine from logic that history is eternal, and that God exists.

> *...He has also set eternity in their heart, yet so that man will not find out the work which God has done from the beginning even to the end. (Ecclesiastes 3:11)*

However, as the second part of the above passage implies, we cannot determine on our own the specifics of what God has done and what He has planned for the future. We need God to tell us these things, which He has indeed done, in the Bible. Science and reasoning enable us determine that God exists, but we need revelation to tell us about eternal life.

Review of book's logical sequence

I have attempted to base this book on principles of evidence, logic, and a reasoned faith. For important and infinite truths, logic and faith also require the use of our imagination for proper insight and understanding.

The general logical progression of the book can be summarized as follows:
1. There is an eternal God who created our universe (Chapters 1 - 5)
    a. It is impossible for "something" to come from "nothing";
    b. There is an eternity-past, with something supernatural (God) always existing;
    c. God brought our temporary physical universe into existence;
    d. Several attributes of God's nature are necessary.
2. An exploration for eternal truth is worthwhile (Chapters 6 - 7)
    a. Ceasing to exist is both empty and terrifying, whereas eternal life is of infinite value and extremely desirable;
    b. Many people have ignored eternity, which obviously prevents them from discovering eternal truth.
3. God has provided a written revelation which is trustworthy for eternal truth (Chapters 8 - 10)
    a. We can only understand eternity-future if God communicates to us;

      b. Faith and imagination are needed to be convinced of and rely on statements about the future;
      c. The Bible has verifiable already-fulfilled prophecies, for which both the prediction and the fulfillment are beyond human ability or accident;
      d. These supernatural predictions provide evidence that the Bible is the place in which God provides revelation of truth;
      e. The Bible can be trusted for its statements of God's intentions and the future.

4. Eternal life is obtained through faith in Jesus Christ (Chapters 11 - 12)
      a. Jesus is the Son of God, and eternal life is in Him;
      b. He voluntarily submitted Himself to execution, and received the punishment for our disobedience to God's rules;
      c. Eternal life is promised to everyone who believes that Jesus died for them, and trusts in Him for forgiveness of disobedience;
      d. The nature of eternal life is both physical and spiritual.

The History and Destiny of the Universe

We have discussed that the appropriate study for the most important questions is the context of the universe in relation to eternity. We have looked at the bigger picture, which includes (1) an infinite amount of time in the past, (2) the creation, duration, and functional collapse of our physical universe, and (3) an infinite amount of time in the future. Our logical and evidential exploration of eternity has given us a glimpse into both the history and future of all things.

History actually has been going on for an infinite amount of time. There is something that has always been, for there could not have been a point in time at which something came from complete nothingness. There was no point at which God began, but He has always been – this is a logical necessity. As for the present, our physical universe did start at a finite point in the past, when it was created by God. Regarding the future, God is eternal and will always exist.

Moreover, each of us can live forever by the power of God, if we meet His condition of faith in His Son, Jesus Christ. There has already been an eternity-past, there will be an eternity-future, and those set the context for our current moment in time.

> *And I am God. Even from eternity I am He*
> *(Isaiah 43:12-13)*
>
> *All things came into being by Him, and apart from Him nothing came into being that has come into being.*
> *(John 1:3)*
>
> *Before the mountains were born or You gave birth to the earth and the world, Even from everlasting to everlasting, You are God.*
> *(Psalm 90:2)*
>
> *Thus declares the Lord who stretches out the heavens, lays the foundation of the earth, and forms the spirit of man within him.*
> *(Zechariah 12:1)*
>
> *For by Him all things were created, both in the heavens and on earth, visible and invisible, whether thrones or dominions or rulers or authorities — all things have been*

> *created through Him and for Him. He is before all things, and in Him all things hold together.*
> *(Colossians 1:16-17)*

The Biblical view of history is eternal, and we have examined this view from a scientific and logical perspective, looking for an intellectual foundation and framework. Fortunately for us, God is not cruel or even neglectful, but has very good intentions for our future and wants to be intimately involved with us.

Eternal life is possible, God desires us to have it, and He has revealed His method. The Son of God gave Himself for us, and faith in Him is the only condition. Jesus' death on the cross is the centerpiece of all history, and opens up eternal life. Rather than stepping into emptiness after death, you have the offer of an eternal future in which each day is filled with love, beauty, and pleasure.

> *The world is passing away, and [also] its lusts; but the one who does the will of God lives forever. (1 John 2:17)*

> *Many of those who sleep in the dust of the ground will awake, these to everlasting life, but the others to disgrace [and] everlasting contempt. (Daniel 12:2)*

The most important aspect of this temporary age is at the individual level, with each person choosing whether to be with God in heaven forever. This life will soon be over, but its choices are eternal. The only true happiness is to live forever, with our family, friends, and God Himself.

Entering Heaven

Once you believe the Bible is true and decide to rely upon Jesus Christ, you can look enthusiastically at the concrete promises of God for the future.

> *Blessed be the God and Father of our Lord Jesus Christ, who according to His great mercy has caused us to be born again to a living hope through the resurrection of Jesus Christ from the dead, <u>to obtain an inheritance which is imperishable and undefiled and will not fade away, reserved in heaven for you</u>, who are protected by the power of God through faith for a salvation ready to be revealed in the last time. In this you greatly rejoice, even though now for a little while, if necessary, you have been distressed by various trials, (1 Peter 1:3-6)*

The passage above highlights that heaven is imperishable, undefiled, and unfading, in contrast to our current corruptible universe. It is also important to put away false misconceptions that heaven is just a concept or a cloudy existence. The Bible emphasizes that it is an actual place which is more real and permanent than anything we have experienced, as Jesus describes below:

> *Do not let your heart be troubled; believe in God, believe also in Me. In My Father's house are many dwelling places; if it were not so, I would have told you; for I go to prepare a place for you. If I go and prepare a place for you, I will come again and receive you to Myself, that where I am, [there] you may be also... (John 14:1-4)*

Because of God's power and the promises of His written revelation, you are able to revolutionize your own view of death and the future. Instead of ceasing to exist upon death, you see that eternal life is obtainable, so that you can experience happiness and pleasure forever. Instead of living now with an intense fear of death, you can look forward to heaven, and set your mind on the fantastic things to come.

If you have placed your faith in Jesus Christ, then you have already been born again spiritually, and in a sense your eternal life has already begun. For the remainder of your current life on earth, you can have an eternal focus, looking forward to what is coming. The eternal God has provided evidence and communicated directly to you, asking you to *"take hold of the eternal life to which you were called" (1 Timothy 6:12).*

Bibliography

Anderson, Sir Robert. *The Coming Prince.* Grand Rapids, Michigan: Kregel Publications, 1957.

Bittinger, Marvin L. *The Faith Equation.* Advantage Books, 2011.

Buchanan, Mark. "The Benefit of the Doubt." *Christianity Today*, April 3, 2000.

Budge, E.A. Wallis. *Babylonian Life And History.* Kessinger Publishing, 2005.

Green, Peter. *Alexander of Macedon 356-323 B.C.: A Historical Biography.* Berkeley, CA: University of California Press, 1991.

Harris, Sam. *The End of Faith.* New York, New York: W.W. Norton & Company, 2005.

"Hartle–Hawking state." *Wikipedia.* April 27, 2012. http://en.wikipedia.org/wiki/Hartle%E2%80%93Hawking_state (accessed June 12, 2012).

Hawking, Stephen W, and Leonard Mlodinow. *The Grand Design.* New York, New York: Bantam Books, 2010.

Josephus, Flavius, and trans. William Whiston. "The Works of Flavius Josephus." *Christian Classics Ethereal Library.* http://www.ccel.org/j/josephus/works/ant-11.htm (accessed June 13, 2012).

McDowell, Josh. *Evidence That Demands a Verdict.* Nashville, Tennessee: Thomas Nelson Publishers, 1979.

Morris, Henry M. *Many Infallible Proofs: Evidences for the Christian Faith.* Green Forest, Arkansas: Master Books, 1996.

Myers, Phillip. *General History for Colleges and High Schools.* Boston: Ginn & Co., 2003.

NASA/WMAP Science Team, National Aeronautics and Space Administration. "Foundations of Big Bang Cosmology." *National Aeronautics and Space Administration.* June 24, 2011. http://map.gsfc.nasa.gov/universe/bb_concepts.html (accessed June 12, 2012).

Nelson, Nina. *Your Guide to Lebanon.* London: Alvin Redman, Ltd., 1965.

Neuhouser, David. *Open to Reason.* Upland, Indiana: Taylor University Press, 2001.

Rufus, Quintus Curtius, and trans. John Yardley. *The History of Alexander.* New York, New York: Penguin, 2001.

Schaeffer, Francis. *The Three Essential Books in One Volume: The God Who Is There, Escape from Reason, He Is There and He Is Not Silent.* Wheaton, Illinois: Crossway Books, 1990.

Shanks, Hershel. *Understanding the Dead Sea Scrolls.* New York: Random House, 1996.

Sproul, R. C. *Christian World View.* Orlando, Florida: Ligonier Ministries, 1988.

—. *Defending Your Faith: An Introduction to Apologetics.* Wheaton, Illinois: Crossway Books, 2003.

—. *The Consequences of Ideas.* Wheaton, Illinois: Crossway Books, 2000.

VanderKam, James, and Peter Flint. *The Meaning of the Dead Sea Scrolls.* San Francisco: Harper Collins, 2004.

Vergano, Dan. "'Universe from Nothing': Big Bang was a bargain." *USA Today*, February 3, 2012.

Notes

Cover

©Public Domain image. National Aeronautics and Space Administration/Ames Research Center, "IRAS imagery Andromeda galaxy from Palomar Observatory," photograph, nasaimages.org, http://archive.org/details/AILS-AC83-0565-2 (accessed July 14, 2012).

©Public Domain image. National Aeronautics and Space Administration/GSFC/NOAA/USGS, " A composite image of the Western hemisphere of the Earth", photograph, wikimedia.org, http://antwrp.gsfc.nasa.gov /apod/image/0304/bluemarble2k_big.jpg (accessed February 1, 2013).

Introduction

[1] (Neuhouser 2001, 7)
[2] Michel de Montaigne, French philosopher, 1533 – 1592.

Chapter 1
The Origin of the Universe

[3] (Harris 2005, 36)
[4] (Hawking and Mlodinow 2010, 155)
[5] (Bittinger 2011, Ebook location 540)
[6] (Hartle–Hawking state 2012)

Chapter 2
Atheism and Eternity-Past

[7] (Hawking and Mlodinow 2010, 162)
[8] (NASA/WMAP Science Team 2011)
[9] (Hawking and Mlodinow 2010, 135)
[10] Lawrence Krauss qtd. in (Vergano 2012)

Chapter 3

A Rational Explanation for the Universe

[11] (Buchanan 2000)

Chapter 7
The Infinite Value of Eternal Life

[12] (Harris 2005, 37)
[13] Woody Allen qtd. in Eric Lax, *On Being Funny: Woody Allen & Comedy* (New York: Manor Books, Inc., 1977)

Chapter 9
The Revelation of Truth

[14] Some key concepts in this chapter were presented by Randy Amos of Rochester, New York, at a Bible conference at Turkey Hill Ranch Bible Camp in Missouri.

Chapter 10
Fulfilled Prophecies

15 ©Public Domain image. Central Intelligence Agency's World Factbook, "Map of Tyre," WikiMedia.org, http://commons.wikimedia.org/wiki/File:Tyre_map.png (accessed June 13, 2012).
[16] (Budge 2005, 50)
[17] ©Public Domain image. Vissarion, "Siege of Tyre based on the ancient authors and aerial photos," WikiMedia.org, http://commons.wikimedia.org/wiki/File:Siege_of_Tyre_332BC_plan.jpg (accessed June 13, 2012).
[18] (Rufus and Yardley 2001, 4.2.3-21)
[19] (Green 1991, 263)
[20] ©Public Domain image. France Air Force, "Aerial photo of Tyre before 1934," photograph, WikiPedia.org, http://en.wikipedia.org/wiki/File:Tyre-aerial-photo-by-France-Military-1934.jpg (accessed June 13, 2012). Published in academic French book "UN GRAND PORT DISPARU T Y R" in 1939, loaded from: almashriq.hiof.no/general/900/930/933/tyr-poidebard/tyr.html.
[21] (Nelson 1965, 220)

[22] (Myers 2003, 55)
[23] (Josephus and Whiston n.d., Book XI, Chapter 8, Section 5)
[24] (Anderson 1957, 66)
[25] (Anderson 1957, 95-97)
[26] (Anderson 1957, 97)

Made in the USA
Columbia, SC
11 August 2017